Adjustment of Adolescents

D0224406

Based on original research carried out in Canberra, Winnipeg, Phoenix, Berlin, Hong Kong, Osaka and Taipei, *Adjustment of Adolescents* examines adolescent adjustment to school, family and friends across cultures. Ruth and William Scott focus on social influences from family, friends and culture as they impinge on the adolescent's personality, attitudinal, demographic and family characteristics. The authors examine the predictors of adjustment of adolescents from different social environments to varying situations, and provide valuable insights into the methodologies of cross-cultural study.

Adjustment of Adolescents will be an ideal resource for undergraduates and masters students undertaking a cross-cultural study, and will make fascinating reading for anyone involved in the study of adolescence.

Ruth Scott is a Visiting Fellow and the late **W. A. Scott** was formerly Emeritus Professor at the Australian National University, Canberra, Australia. Their previous publications include *Adaptation of Immigrants: Individual Differences and Determinations* (1989).

INTERNATIONAL SERIES IN SOCIAL PSYCHOLOGY
Series Editor: Professor W. Peter Robinson, University of Bristol, UK

If you wish to contribute to the series please send a synopsis to Professor Peter Robinson, University of Bristol, Department of Psychology, 8 Woodlands Road, Bristol BS8 1TN.

NATIONAL UNIVERSITY
LIBRARY   SAN DIEGO

Adjustment of Adolescents

Cross-cultural similarities and differences

Ruth Scott and W. A. Scott

London and New York

First published 1998
by Routledge
11 New Fetter Lane, London EC4P 4EE

Simultaneously published in the USA and Canada
by Routledge
29 West 35th Street, New York, NY 10001

© 1998 Ruth Scott and W. A. Scott

Typeset in Times by
Jayvee, Trivandrum, India
Printed and bound in Great Britain by
Biddles Ltd, Guildford and King's Lynn

All rights reserved. No part of this book may be reprinted or reproduced or utilised in any form or by any electronic, mechanical, or other means, now known or hereafter invented, including photocopying and recording, or in any information storage or retrieval system, without permission in writing from the publishers.

British Library Cataloguing in Publication Data
A catalogue record for this book is available from the British Library

Library of Congress Cataloging in Publication Data
A catalogue record for this book has been requested

ISBN 0-415-18533-5 (pbk)
ISBN 0-415-18532-7 (hbk)

Contents

Preface and Acknowledgements

This book brings together the results of our 1986–7 study of adolescent adjustment in seven cultures. The data are based on questionnaires from high school students, their parents, teachers, and fellow class-mates in schools located in Canberra, Winnipeg, Phoenix, Berlin, Hong Kong, Osaka, and Taipei. The main aim of the research was to examine the antecedents of adjustment of adolescents to varying situations (school, family and friends) as viewed by themselves, their parents, teachers and classmates.

The monograph focuses on the socio-demographic characteristics and social influences from family, friends and culture as they impinge on the adolescent's coping mechanisms. The problems of interpreting cross-cultural similarities and differences are addressed in detail, as are the issues in analyzing data that is obtained from more than one source. The emphasis is on multivariate analysis and cross-cultural validation of relationships found within each sample. Hopefully this will point the way for more research using different sources in contrasting cultures.

We have built on the 20th century research of many people in fields once considered diverse: sociology and anthropology, social, and cross-cultural psychology. The major ones that have influenced our thinking are referred to throughout this book, and to them we say thank you. In addition, we have used questions from many researchers, also acknowledged throughout the book. This research drew upon our own previous work. In a longitudinal study of the adjustment of Australian migrant children, it became clear that school meant different things to different cultures, and that led to our desire to enquire into the differential effects of the social environment, including culture on adjustment.

Many contribute to any research endeavour. I would particularly like to mention the Australian Research Council and the Division of Psychology at the Australian National University. In addition to the collaborators in the various cities; Klaus Boehnke, Masamichi Sasake and Kwok Leung and the late Shall-Way Chen, the research would not have been possible in Phoenix without the help of John Reich and John Adair in Winnipeg. And, of course, all the school authorities, principals, teachers, students and their parents played major roles in bringing this work to fruition. The promise of anonymity means that they cannot be thanked personally in public.

On a more personal level, since the death of my husband in 1991, I have received support from many individuals in my endeavour to see this book published. A special thanks to Cindy Gallois and Debbie Terry at the University of Queensland, and Valerie Braithwaite of the Australian National University for reading every word of a earlier draft, and offering concrete suggestions on how to make improvements. Thanks also to Susan Smithson who proof read every page at the end. Further, appreciation to Don Byrne, John Turner and the members of the Division of Psychology here at the Australian National University at all levels, for office space, computer support, intellectual stimulus and collegiate encouragement; and to Peter Robinson, the editor of this series, who has been supportive since he first heard I was planning to complete the book on my own. Finally, thanks to all my colleagues and friends throughout the world who encouraged me. Of those not mentioned above, a special thank you to Brewster Smith and former colleagues from our University of Colorado days, O. J. Harvey, Ron Johnson and Dick Jessor. Last but not least, I would like to thank my family, who constantly nagged at me until this book was finished.

Ruth Scott
Australian National University

1

Background and Overview

One of the major challenges facing those living in technologically advanced societies is the need to adjust to various, and sometimes conflicting, social systems such as the family, friendship networks, work or school groups, and various traditional groups including the church which are oriented toward preserving cultural norms. At adolescence, the conflict among the demands of several groups is likely to be particularly acute, as increasingly autonomous children struggle to gain freedom from parents, to meet teachers' demands for academic performance, to make and maintain friendships, and to find a place for themselves in society. For the most part, the family and the school are allied in their expectation of increasing social maturity through internalizing adult values. In contrast, the adolescent peer group may exert pressures antagonistic to these adult institutions, perhaps because children want more control over their own lives and judge the peer group to be more similar to themselves, and therefore more sympathetic to their interests, than the adult-dominated social order (Bronfenbrenner, 1970; Coleman, 1961).

What effect do these various demands have on the adolescent? Can we predict adolescents' adjustment to their various areas of concern, which in this book include academic matters, interpersonal concerns and family relations? Do different judges (the self, parents, teachers, peers) evaluate the success of adjustment similarly? Are factors contributing to a successful adjustment in one situation, say the family, the same as those in another area? Finally, do these associations of adjustment generalize across cultures? These are the questions addressed in this book. Data have been collected on the adjustment of adolescents in seven different cultures. The general model posits that environmental conditions result in the individual adopting coping styles that subsequently shape his or her adjustment. In this chapter we will discuss the theoretical rationale for the model and the definitions of the environmental conditions, coping styles and adjustment outcomes, along with the previous work on which they are based.

Before we do this, a number of distinctive features about this broad gauge, cross-cultural research warrant discussion. First, this book proposes a psychologically integrated, as opposed to a compartmentalized, approach. Second, it pursues transcultural stability as the criterion for establishing variables as major predictors of adolescent adjustment. Third, it examines the adjustment of adolescents over different areas of concern, as seen not only through their own eyes, but also through the eyes of their significant others: parents, teachers and peers.

Figure 1.1 outlines our model. It also specifies the chapters in which each particular classification of variables is introduced. We will briefly present the measures we used to represent these concepts, as well as the work of others we used to guide our selection of variables. All descriptive data entered into our models are based on mean within-sample results collected from seven cities representing both Occidental and Oriental cultures, described in full in Chapter 2, and include the data from four perspectives: the child, his/her parent, teacher and classmates. All relational data are based on the total sample when the contribution of specific cultures has been partialled out.

Starting with Chapter 3, we describe the adjustment data, their interrelationships, and their relationship with the coping styles which we predict mediate the effect of the various classes of predictors. Though in this book we are emphasizing the gains that can be made by an integrative approach to data analysis, we introduce each type of data by first establishing the zero-order effects on our outcome adjustment measures and coping variables. This is followed by presenting their unique effects, represented by their *beta* weights in multiple regression analyses containing other significant predictors. Chapter 4 describes the effect of the significant demographic variables on the mediating and dependent variables. This is followed by the family variables, introduced into the model in Chapter 6 after being described in detail in Chapter 5, the peer variables (Chapter 7) and, finally the cultural variables in Chapter 8.

Adjustment Evaluated By Whom: The Source Effect

Success of the adjustment to social systems can be appraised both subjectively and objectively. By subjective adjustment we mean self-judged satisfaction with a particular domain of life; for adolescents, the three main foci for adjustment are defined as school, friends and family. By objective adjustment we mean the adequacy of the role performance in that domain, as judged by role partners. Adjustment to school may be appraised both as subjective satisfaction and, objectively, by others' evaluations of the student's academic performance. Adjustment to friends can be measured as subjective satisfaction with interpersonal relations, and objectively, by acceptance by others and their evaluations of the adolescents' competence in these roles. Finally, adjustment to family can be represented both as satisfaction with other members and as their reciprocated satisfaction with the adolescent.

This study is distinctive in its attempt to map both the subjective and the objective adjustment of adolescents and the degree of similarity in their predictors

Antecedents ——→ Mediators (coping styles) ——→ Outcomes (Adjustments to:)

Demographics (Chapter 4)

Of child
Sex, age verbal ability (C)[a]
Mark(S)

Of parent
Sex, Age, Education (P)

Of family
Minority group (C,P)
Number of parents, children (C,P)

Family relations (Chapters 5 and 6)

Parental practices
Nurturance (C,P)
Protectiveness (C,P)
Punitiveness (C,P)

Role allocation
Status, Maintenance roles (C,P)
Sex, age differentiation, concentration (C,P)

Peer measures (Chapter 7)
Similarity to child's score (F: C,P,T)
Means (F: C,P,T)

Cultural Norms (Chapter 8)
Means (F: C,P,T)
Unspecified Variance

Personality (Chapter 3)
Self-esteem (C,T)
Anxiety (C,P,T)
Hostility (C,P,T)

Meaning of school (Chapter 3)
School means study (C,P)

School
Subjective (C)
Satisfaction
Academic performance

Objective (role performance (P,T)
Academic performance

Friends
Subjective (C)
Satisfaction
Interpersonal comfort
Number of friends chosen

Objective (role performance)
Interpersonal competence (T)
Sociometric ratings (F)

Family
Subjective (C)
Satisfaction with

Objective (role performance (P)
Satisfaction with
Satisfaction with child's behaviour

Sources: C = Child; P = Parent; T = Teacher; F = Peers

[a]

FIGURE 1.1   Adolescent adjustment model: specification and classification of measures.

using data collected from diverse sources; the child, the parent, the teacher and classmates. In general, there is a tendency toward convergence between subjective and objective adaptation within any particular domain. People who are performing well are likely to receive favourable feedback from their role partners, which enhances their self-esteem, and hence their satisfaction with the role system. Conversely, satisfaction with one's colleagues in a role system is likely to encourage effort to perform to their satisfaction. A complementary reciprocity is likely to prevail among dissatisfied, inadequately performing members of a group as well. Negatively valued members tend to give up their role obligations, which further increases their alienation from the group.

Adjustment to What: Situational Determinants

The terms adaptation and adjustment imply not only an adapting person, but a set of circumstances which impose demands and requirements. One adapts to school, to a wartime battlefield, to parenthood, to a poker club. To say that one becomes better adjusted risks a confusion between the individual and the situational component. The capacity to adapt to a wide range of situations may, indeed, facilitate success in numerous endeavours, but we find it clearer to conceive such a capacity as an aspect of personality, which provides only one part of the adaptive process. The other part, situational characteristics, is a necessary ingredient as well. It is quite easy to imagine a circumstance—such as oxygenless atmosphere or a totally unpredictable social environment—with which even the most hardy (adaptable) person could not cope. We conceive of adjustment as the contribution of the individual to adaptation that can be viewed by the self or others in a specific domain of activity.

While acknowledging that success generalizes to new areas of life and failure demoralizes, inhibiting or disorganizing action in other domains as well as the focal one, we assume at the outset a fair degree of domain specificity. In other words, it is quite possible for a person to do well in one area of life and poorly in others. Moreover, this conceptualization allows for the practice of individuals' transferring effort and attention from the less to the more successful domains, thereby expanding their attention to new areas which look promising.

Adjustment Where: Cultural Contributions

Finally, the contribution of the culture in which the adolescent is embedded also plays a part in the child's adjustment, both as viewed by the child and by role partners, such as family members, peers and teachers. By culture we mean the shared meanings among the individual members of the social groups as displayed by their expressed opinions and behaviours. It is now common to measure and compare opinions and behaviours across cultures, but the fact that there are rarely large numbers of cultures sampled limits the inferences that can be drawn from the data. Further limitations result from the use of opportunistic rather than theory-based selection techniques when picking the subjects. Within cultures, the use of equal-probability samples is rare, with university students usually the only population from which subjects are chosen. Differential restrictions between samples (cultures) have consequences for inter-cultural comparisons. One cannot infer an underlying basis for differences between two samples when the differences lie only in responses to specific scales or on the relationship between two variables, as there are too many other differences between the two societies, measured and unmeasured, that could also be the cause. However, if there is a common predictive model found within various cultures and these differences are also mirrored in mean differences between samples, then we are on firmer ground in interpreting cultural differences (see Scott, Scott, Boehnke, Cheng, Leung and Sasaki, 1991).

Here, we will first develop models predicting adjustment which hold within our seven cultures before examining the role cultural differences may play in influencing levels of adjustment. For instance, in our study, the very important relationship between high parental nurturance and high self-esteem scores is found within each sample. This finding also holds when comparing cultures; cultures with high mean parental-nurturance scores also have high self-esteem scores, as reported by the adolescents. This leads us to say that the cultural differences in self-esteem, an important mediator for subjective and objective school and friend adjustment, are based on cultural differences in parental nurturance.

Theoretical Framework: An Integrative Approach

Recently, there has been a trend to simplify research design and topics: to look at a single domain of predictors (e.g. friendship groups) with data collected from a single source (e.g. self-report) from one group of subjects (e.g. university students). Though undoubtedly this is in part a result of a need to refine theory and instruments, it is also driven by the need to publish in order to get promotion or a new grant. Even when databases exist allowing examination of many variables from more than one source, information about non-predicted variables, including those driven by instrument design (scale type and direction), are treated as extraneous noise, contributing to an increased error term, rather than as something which could add to the understanding of the outcome under study. Of course, longitudinal studies, or those requiring data collection from more than one source of subjects and more than one type of sample, require a time perspective beyond the reach of many current researchers.

In his 1936 book *Topological Psychology*, Kurt Lewin presented his formula for predicting behaviour as a function of personality and environment. Along with Cattell (1993) and the MacArthur Foundation Research Network on

Successful Adolescent Development, as reported by Jessor (1993), in this book we first call for a return to an integrative approach to research, whereby we increase our understanding of the relative influence of various domains of variables on predicting behaviour. Second, we hope this project will rekindle emphasis on the methodological effects of instrument construction, data source, and sample selection on designing studies (see Chen, Lee and Stevenson, 1995). Further, we hope this book will lead to more replication of relationships found within one culture to those in others. Most of the frameworks now driving social psychological research have been developed within the industrial Western culture, primarily the United States. Do these frameworks also predict behaviour in other, non-Capitalistic, non-Judaeo-Christian cultures? Would other variables increase the ability to predict behaviour in Oriental cultures? These are the questions one hopes future researchers will be addressing in greater numbers.

Overall Objectives

This study was designed to test the universality of the effects of the individual's coping behaviour as driven by demographic characteristics and influences from his/her social environment to specific situations. Adjustment is by definition an overt achievement more or less discernible to other people, whereas personality is an inferred construct, even for the behaving individual, and, therefore, is less likely to be similarly appraised by various sources. Following Baron and Kenny (1986), we assume that coping styles, here represented as personality and general orientation, mediate the effects of the four major domains of predictors. By that, we mean that demographic variables, along with family, peer and cultural characteristics, influence the coping styles of the child, which in turn affect her/his adjustment to specific situations, at school, with friends, and at home with the family.

Our overriding aim was to bring together into one study the predictors of adolescent adjustment identified in restricted research contexts by people working in various areas, in order to test their comparative strength and their combined contributions in understanding adolescent adjustment. Using our typology to structure these predictors (demographic or specific social environment), we have developed a model to drive our analyses which assumes more than one type of data, more than one source of information, more than one situation in which adjustment applies, and more than one sample. Particular attention was paid to measurement effects, by varying the wording of questions and the direction of response as much as possible. Data were solicited from more than one source, so that the conclusions could either be shown to generalize across observers or to be specific to the person doing the observing. Using the same predictors, we were able to compare their generality or specificity across situations. Finally, in gathering information from more than one sample, we could replicate the findings, as well as point to the influence of the largest social environmental network in this study, the general culture or nation on the adaptation process.

Specifically, the five objectives of the project were:

1. To ascertain relations among measures of adolescent adjustment to three domains: school, friends and family; using parent, teacher and peer assessment, in addition to self-report. This assumes that the source of ratings of adjustment to a specific situation will be determined by different predictors, though there will be a positive relationship between adjustment ratings in the same domain. Outcome measures based on different raters have normally been treated as noise or error in measurement of the same underlying latent variable. Here we assume that same domain outcome variables reflect models with different antecedents. For example, though the child's self-reported degree of satisfaction with school is associated with his/her judgement of academic performance, it is a different aspect of the general domain of academic adjustment, as it has some different predictors (see Chapter 4, Figure 4.1).

2. To test the proposed model which we imposed on our data: that the effects on adjustment in a particular situation (academic, interpersonal or family) are mediated by an overall predisposition to appropriate coping behaviour. This rests on our distinction between a general, overall style of adapting to the various demands of the environment and the relative success or failure of the outcome (adjustment) depending on the relationship between the demands of the situation and the coping styles of the individual.

3. To identify predictors of adjustment from the demographic characteristics of the adolescents.

4. To establish the relative importance of influences from the adolescent's social environment, here represented by variables from the family, their classroom friends and cultural norms.

5. To establish relationships within all seven samples drawn from urban youth in seven industrialized countries, as a means of understanding cross-cultural differences.

The Model

Figure 1.1 also introduces our variables into the model used in our study. These are classified as outcome variables, antecedents, and mediators. Outcomes (column 3) are adjustment to the three foci discussed above: school, friends and family, as judged by the self and others.

Mediating variables (column 2) are the three personality characteristics: self-esteem, anxiety and hostility, plus the child's cognitive appraisal of school means study. A number of different meanings were tapped; those of particular concern here are academic and discipline on the one hand, friendship and recreation on the other. By designating these mediating variables, the implication is that the effects of all antecedent variables operate through the mediators, and these effects will disappear when the mediators are included in the analyses.

Antecedents (column 1) include the demographic variables, and aspects of family relations, characteristics of the children's friends, and cultural norms. In all analyses, we will be looking at the direct and mediated effects of these antecedents, to ascertain the extent to which the proposed model applies: namely, that all antecedents operate through the hypothesized mediators. Our method of analysis, as noted above, is relatively unusual. However, using an approach analogous to ours in another domain, Scherer and colleagues (Scherer, 1988; Scherer, Wallbott and Summerfield, 1986), in their research on facets of emotion, looked for cross-cultural similarities and differences in the response of university students (single source), using a theory-driven model which classified variables as antecedents, experiences, expressions and consequences.

Now to a review of our concepts, accompanied by a brief review of the literature upon which their selection is based. A detailed description of the operational definitions of all variables, along with their source and data descriptions, will be deferred until they are introduced into the model. Starting with the third column, we will first look at the variables selected to measure the adjustment outcomes.

Outcome Variables of Adjustment

Academic adjustment

Academic adjustment can be subdivided into many components: satisfaction with school, attendance and persistence, competence in teachers' eyes, achievement measures, liking by teachers, teacher-judged adjustment to school, and reaction to authority, to name just a few. Previous research shows a general tendency for various measures of academic adjustment to be positively intercorrelated. For instance, high scholastic performance is linked to socially appropriate behaviour as reported by teachers of Quebec high-school students (Loranger, Verret and Arsenault, 1986), and teachers' ratings of children's school adjustment were found by Takac and Benyamini (1989) to be substantially correlated with school-appropriate behaviour. Teachers appear especially sensitive to students' behaviour as an indicator of their adjustment.

Teachers in grades 7—12 of a North Carolina high school judged students with acting-out problems to be more in need of special attention than students who were shy, anxious, or withdrawn (Wall and Pryzwansky, 1985), whereas no such distinction was made by mental-health professionals. Obedient middle-school children in India were better adjusted, according to teachers' ratings, than disobedient children (also assessed from teachers' ratings, Mehta, 1983). Among 14- and 15-year-olds, but not among 12-year-olds in Poland, teacher-judged emotional and social maturity were associated with (teacher-rated) positive attitudes toward authority (Cierkonski, 1975).

There are some exceptions, nevertheless, to this tendency toward generality of adjustment level. No differences were found in teacher-rated adjustment of high and low achieving students of science, agricultural science, and agricultural engineering schools in an Indian university (Kumawat, 1985), while a study of 80 Indian high-school students aged 13–14 (Bharadwaj, 1985) found no correlation between personal adjustment and their scientific achievement.

For our study, we choose academic performance as judged by the teacher, parent and the child him/herself, in addition to the child's general satisfaction with school. We left school marks as an independent predictor, rather than an outcome component, as it, along with a measure of verbal ability, also represents the antecedent intelligence, a predictor of achievement.

Interpersonal adjustment

Social adjustment has been broadly defined in terms of subjective measures (satisfaction with one's friends) and objective measures (acceptance by one's peers). There is some evidence that the social and academic adjustment of students are positively related. For instance, reading and mathematics achievement scores were positively correlated with students' levels of social initiation, cooperation and peer reinforcement (Clark, Gresham and Elliott, 1985). On the other hand, among Israeli children 10 to 12 years of age, school adjustment, as rated by teachers, was generally independent of peer adjustment (Takac and Benyamini, 1989).

As with academic adjustment, interpersonal adjustment was also divided into sub-categories. These are self-reported satisfaction with friends, interpersonal competence as viewed by self and teachers, and popularity with others as reported by classmates and self.

Family adjustment

Family adjustment has been assessed as children's satisfaction with their families and the degree of friendly contact maintained with parents (Olson, McCubbin, Barnes, Larson, Muxen and Wilson, 1983; Scott and Scott, 1989). These measures have ordinarily been found to correlate positively with each other, as one would expect from subjective measures of family relations. In addition, family adjustment measures have been found to be associated with school adjustment, not surprising as both situations emphasize conformity to the adult world. The association with peer adjustment is less clear, and, perhaps, reflects the divergent demands of the role of family and peer group member (Scott and Scott, 1989).

So, even family adjustment has its sub-parts. In addition to satisfaction with family through the student's eyes, parental satisfaction with family and parental judgment of child's behaviour, were selected. Chapter 3 will describe the resulting twelve adjustment measures and their interrelationship.

Mediating Variables

We are hypothesizing that social and demographic variables have only an indirect effect on the child's adjustment. That is, when the effects of the intervening variables are included in the same model, the direct relationship between antecedents and outcomes will disappear. If children's academic performance depends on their sex, then the psychologist looks for personality concomitants of sex that can explain the association. If the child's interpersonal relations with peers depend on the family constellation, the relationship would be clarified by describing the mechanisms by which the family influence the child's coping styles (i.e. parental nurturance leading to greater self-esteem) and thereby, his/her interpersonal competence.

Adjustment associated with personality

Berry and Kim (1988) define mental health as "effective functioning in daily life and the ability to deal with new situations" (p. 119). It is within this framework that we define personality as a coping style implemented when dealing with external demands, in our case school, friends, or family (see Berry, 1980, who uses this in interpreting migrant adaptation). In our model, measures of "general personal adjustment," including overall life satisfaction, teacher-judged emotional maturity, and objective tests of neuroticism and related traits, are defined as personality measures reflecting coping styles, not measures of adjustment, as no situational locus of adaptation is specified.

There is considerable evidence for positive correlations among these kinds of personality traits and specific adjustment measures for students of whatever age, including high-school students, the subjects of this study. For instance, high anxiety was associated with poor school performance, poor attendance and conflict with teachers and friends among high-school students in Poland (Cierkonski, 1975). Use of the university counselling centre, assumed to be an objective measure of low school adjustment, was associated with level of neuroticism, anxiety, life satisfaction, and self-esteem (Estes, 1973; McClure, Mitchell and Greschuck, 1982), and, at a Canadian university, students were found to display more personal problems and lower self-esteem than non-users (Poirier, Tetreau and Strobel, 1979). Personal adjustment among college students (low levels of anxiety, depression and alcohol use) was associated with high quality of peer relations and communication with their roommates (Waldo, 1984).

One of the most important adaptive coping styles is the personality trait, self-esteem, with its effect on academic achievement widely established in different cultures. Abadzi (1984), using a modified Coopersmith (1967) model of self-esteem antecedents on fourth-grade students, found a correlation of .34 between self-esteem and academic achievement. Longitudinal data in Norway highlight the correlation between academic achievement and self-esteem in elementary school classes (Skaalvik and Hagtvet, 1990). Youngblood (1976), with 907 Filipino high school students, and Bahr and Martin (1983) also showed that self-esteem had a strong association with academic achievement and family solidarity (similar to our family satisfaction).

A persuasive study by McClure (1974) attempted to predict adjustment problems among 697 students in an American college from a battery of tests subjected to multiple-discriminant analysis. Three canonical variates were identified, associated with the personality characteristics of neuroticism, introversion and hostility. Scores on these components predicted counselling-centre attendance and adjustment problems for a second group of 187 first- and second-year students.

Among these intervening personality variables considered in explaining children's adjustment to specific situations, those selected for this study were the individual characteristics of self-esteem (Coopersmith, 1967), anxiety (Taylor, 1953) and hostility (Caine, Foulds and Hope, 1967).

Adjustment associated with orientation

In addition to personality as a measure of adjustment coping styles, the relative salience of the situation to which the individual must adapt was examined. The perception that school means study (in contrast to friends) was included on the basis of previous results showing that children's satisfaction with school was uncorrelated, or even negatively correlated, with their academic performance (see Scott and Scott, 1989, 1991). From this it was suspected that school could have several different meanings to children, academic performance and establishing interpersonal contacts representing two major ones.

Antecedents of Adjustment and Coping Styles

Specific antecedent variables were selected with an aim of covering all domains to which potentially theoretically salient variables belong. The important variables for predicting adjustment can be categorized as belonging to the physical or background variables and those describing the social environment of the child: family, classmates and culture (see column 1 Figure 1.1). Below we review the

literature covering the demographic variables we deemed to be important predictors of adjustment and the coping styles which the adolescent might use in
adaptation.

Demographic correlates

Sex

Epstein and McPartland (1977b) found few significant sex differences in adaptation of 4079 middle- and high-school students, when the effects of other variables in their study were partialled out. Only in self-esteem did boys score
significantly differently from girls (higher), while females tended to receive higher grades, when the effects of intelligence and other measured variables were
partialled out, and males were more likely to be involved in discipline problems.
The number of significant interactions of sex with other predictors of academic
adjustment was no more than would be expected by chance. These authors con-
cluded, therefore, that the determinants of adjustment were similar for boys and
girls. Further, Ohannessian, Lerner, Lerner and von Eye (1994) found no difference in the relationship between reports on family adjustment and several measures of emotional adjustment, including self-worth, which we would equate to
our coping style measure of self-esteem.

In a sample of Black undergraduate students from six predominantly White universities, Allen (1988) found males to be more socially involved than females and
to have higher occupational aspirations. Berndt, Miller and Park (1989) found that
seventh-grade girls tended to like school better than boys and be more involved in
it, while boys were more tolerant than girls of classroom misbehaviour. The first of
these findings was echoed in Williamson's (1977) study of senior high-school students in Pennsylvania: Girls tended to be more satisfied with school than boys.
Levine (1977) found that both male and female primary-school teachers were
likely to rate girls as better adjusted than boys. Both teachers and the pupils
themselves rated secondary-school girls in Montreal and Quebec higher in suitable
deportment than boys (Loranger, Verret, and Arsenault, 1986).

Wagner and Compas (1990) found girls reporting more negative events than
boys in samples taken from junior high schools, senior high schools and colleges;
for both high school samples these were reflected in girls indicating more interpersonal stresses than boys. Frankenhauser (1983) reported that demands for
achievement were more likely to result in anxiety for males, whereas stresses
were more likely to be associated with anxiety in females. Furnham and Gunter
(1989) in a study in the UK and Darom and Rich (1988) in a study in Israel found
more positive attitudes toward school (equivalent to our orientation concept) for
girls than for boys, with Darom and Rich further reporting more negative
attitudes towards boys on the part of teachers.

Age

The pattern of adolescent–parent conflict was summarized by Petersen (1988) in her review of adolescent development. These conflicts are associated with other manifestations of maladjustment. In spite of indicators of self-esteem becoming more positive with age of adolescents (Damon and Hart, 1982), behavioural indicators of malaise, such as suicide, also increased for this age group (Petersen and Hamburg, 1986).

Age of child (measured by enrolled grade in school, between sixth and twelfth) was a major negative correlate of three aspects of white children's adjustment to Maryland schools (Epstein and McPartland, 1977b). The older the children, the less their satisfaction with the school, the more disruptive their (self-reported) behaviour, and the lower their marks (report-card grades). Greater disaffection with age may be due in part to the child's increasing desire for autonomy coupled with a sense of decreasing freedom of choice in the school system (Midgley and Feldlaufer, 1987).

Intelligence

Using global measures of adjustment or coping styles, Raphael (1988) found, in an American sample of 90 twelfth-grade girls, that their satisfaction with themselves (a parallel concept to self-esteem) and their circumstances was correlated, to a small degree, with intelligence and, to a considerably higher degree, with conceptual level (CL) assessed with a paragraph-completion test which is purported to assess the complexity of information search and categorization typically displayed by the subject (Hunt, Butler, Noy and Rosser, 1977). Pandey (1977) reports that, among a sample of 200 intermediate-school boys in Uttar Pradesh, India, those who scored higher on two intelligence tests also showed higher than average scores on a social adjustment component, but there were no significant differences on home, health and emotional adjustment.

In a study of 223 below average New Zealand children 14–17 years old, Ryba, Edelman and Chapman (1984) found self-report tests pertaining to the student's ability, self-concept, and social skills showed generally positive intercorrelations, averaging around .25, between ability and social relations measures. In Allen's (1988) study of Black students (see above), high-school grades constituted the largest relative contributor to college academic achievement, represented by a *beta*-coefficient (standardized regression coefficient) of .24; no other predictor came close to this one in predictive power.

Minority-group status

In the United States, the effect of race on academic adjustment has received particular attention. It has been found, for example, that Black students, who attend predominantly White schools, tend to drop out more readily, to do less well scholastically, and feel incapable of meeting the academic requirements imposed upon them, in comparison with their White or Asian students (Allen, 1988). Furthermore, Oliver, Rodriguez and Mickelson (1985) found that Blacks felt more alienated and did less well academically than their Chicano counterparts.

Family composition

The simplest bases for distinguishing among families have to do with their composition, usually meaning the number of adults and the number and sex of children. Yet these variables have not accounted for much variance in children's personalities or adaptation. Single- and two-parent families do not differ dependably in the academic adjustment of their children, either in college (Lopez, 1987) or in elementary and secondary school (Emery, 1982; Mechanic and Hansell, 1989; Slater and Haber, 1984). In spite of the lack of support, we retained the variables representing the number of people in the family along with the demographic characteristics of the parents, such as their age and education. We have classified them here, rather than under family relations, which we limit to characteristics of the social environment of the family.

Summary

In summary, those demographic variables selected and introduced in Chapter 4 are the sex and age of the child, along with his/her school grades or marks and a verbal ability test score. Demographic characteristics of the responding parent were his/her sex, age and educational level. Finally, composition of the family, represented by the number of adults and number of children along with minority group membership were categorized as demographic characteristics of the child's family.

Family characteristics

"Family relations" is a general term referring to family members' routine ways of dealing with each other. Sometimes the term "family dynamics" is employed, but neither of these terms specifies the variables any more clearly. There have been few attempts to describe formally these modes of interpersonal conduct so that they can be related systematically to any particular outcome. One may speak of the "quality of family life" without specifying any particular dimension of quality; no doubt there are several. Boehnke (1996) uses the term "family climate," which he defines as "a global construct used to describe the current, but fairly stable properties of a family environment with regard to (a) the ecological context of a family, (b) the structural properties of a family, (c) the quality of relations within the family, (d) the expectations and aspirations of a family, (e) the educational orientation of parents, and (f) the personalities of the family members" (pp. 14–15). Before defining our measures, we will review other definitions of family characteristics along with their findings.

Parental practices presumably exercise potent influences on their children's development. Hypotheses about the effects of the family on the child's ability to adapt have developed out of two main theoretical frameworks. The first, symbolic interactionism (Cheek and Hogan, 1983; Cooley, 1922; Mead, 1934) is based on the notion that self-esteem (then called the self-concept) was the reflection of powerful others, in this case parents. The second is learning theory, as exemplified by Bandura (1977) and Miller and Dollard (1941), which proposes that subordinates, children in our case, learn methods of coping by imitating role models of a powerful other, (e.g. a parent). In both cases, parental practices and family role dispersion would be predicted to have a powerful influence on the ability of children to cope with school, interpersonal relations and the family itself.

Hammen, Burge and Stansbury (1990) propose a model that shows parent–child interaction as a mediator of parents' and children's maladjustment in affecting the child's symptoms. Their clearest relations displayed in the table of intercorrelations among components of the latent variables are between the child's social competence and behaviour problems (self-report), and the mother's depression score. Similar correlations have been reported elsewhere (Rutter, 1990), but the interpersonal mechanisms by which maternal characteristics are transmitted to the child remain unclear. Among the most likely are low responsiveness of the mother to the infant child's behaviour (Goodman and Brumley, 1990). Unfortunately for our purposes, most of these observational studies were directed toward infants rather than adolescents, so one can only infer that mothering processes found in infancy are continuous through adolescence or that parental effects in infancy are important for the outcomes in adolescence.

Compas, Howell, Phares, Williams and Ledoux (1989) found a complex set of relations between parents' and adolescents' symptoms. Their study of around 200 adolescents and their parents in Vermont, found higher correlations between parents' stresses and symptoms than between parents' and children's scores on these variables, which were nevertheless significant for fathers and children. The authors interpret their data to show that both boys' and girls' behaviour problems were affected by their fathers', but not their mothers', psychological symptoms. However, alternative interpretations—for example, that children's behaviour problems exacerbated fathers' neurotic symptoms—were not precluded. The latter direction of effect is implicit in Silverberg and Steinberg's (1990) study of adolescents' signs of maturity (heterosocial involvement, persuasive reasoning skills and physiological puberty) in relation to their parents' emotional wellbeing. The main finding was that parents involved in their work appeared to be less upset by these adolescent manifestations than were less work-oriented parents. In other words, the effect of family relations on members depends on the extent of their extra-family relations as well. These studies led us to narrow our areas of concern to two family relation categories, parental practices and family roles.

Parental practices

Recently, investigators have been trying to specify just what it is about family relations that may be affected by single parenting or multiple and mixed-sex siblings or psychiatric disability of the parent. A single parent may tend to become either negligent or over-protective. The lone child may suffer either from over- or under-stimulation, and it is these mediating processes that are of interest here. Early research by Sears, Maccoby and Levin (1957) and Cooper-smith (1967) emphasized the relationship between parental warmth or nurturance and the child's self-esteem, while the McCord, McCord and Howard (1961) studies detailed the association between the child's hostility and parental punitiveness. Gordon Parker and his colleagues (Parker, 1983, 1989; Parker and Barnett, 1988) have focused on two properties, called "care" and "overprotection", using Parker's Parental Bonding Instrument (PBI; Parker, Tupling and Brown, 1979). The first of these includes our "nurturance" variable, and we have used items from their scale. Likewise, items from overprotection have been included in our parental protectionism scale. No specific circumstance of adaptation is implied by Parker; rather the dependent variables have mostly been various forms of psychiatric illness, such as schizophrenia and depression, which, within our schema, might be regarded as more akin to personality characteristics than to adaptive outcomes in a particular environment.

McCrae and Costa (1988a, 1988b) found substantial agreement between the ratings of mother and the ratings of father on "parenting." They also found nurturance to have a direct effect on subjective satisfaction, but not on behaviour, and that this effect was not mediated completely through the personality variables, with which it had only modest correlations. Sarason, Sarason and Shearin (1986) found that retrospective reports of parental nurturance and overprotection by university students contributed significantly to predictions of social satisfaction. Steinberg, Elmen and Mounts (1989) found parental warmth and control as contributing to academic achievement.

A limitation of the measures of parental style is that it depends mainly on recall of family relations by the person whose current state (e.g. schizophrenic) is being assessed, rather than on independent appraisal of those relations. Although there was some evidence of agreement between siblings or twins in several studies (Parker, 1989) concerning treatment received from their parents ($\underline{r}$s ranged between .10 and .71 for various samples), there is still insufficient work to show that parental style, *independently assessed*, predicts personality or adaptive outcomes ascertained from the focal subject or some other distinct source (Mackinnon, Henderson and Andrews, 1991).

Youngblood (1976) used a family authority scale to distinguish "firm but loving" families and found that it, along with high socioeconomic status and self-esteem, predicted scholastic achievement among Filipino high school students. Epstein and McPartland (1977a) have focused on a different pair of family characteristics, "status" and "process." The first of these refers to a jumble of family size, parents' education and material possessions, while the latter consists of two components, student participation in family decision-making and level of regulation imposed on the student. Measures for these properties are obtained from the student only, and are therefore subject to the same kinds of biases as are Parker's. In addition, their measures of adjustment refer to academic success, school coping skills (which we classify as outcome measures, namely school satisfaction and satisfactory behaviour), and aspirations for further education.

In Epstein and McPartland's (1977a, 1977b) study of 4079 middle- and high-school White students in Maryland, USA, family status was substantially related only to academic aspirations and standardized achievement scores. Students' participation in family decision-making was positively related to their school satisfaction and deportment, as well as to several of their personality variables (our classification): self-reliance, self-esteem, (low) anxiety, (low) hostility, and sense of efficacy. Finally, family regulation of the child was related (negatively) to school satisfaction and deportment. Amato (1990) used multi-dimensional scaling to analyse children's perceptions of family and proposed support and control as the two most important dimensions.

Our summary of the literature led us to concentrate on the variables representing parental nurturance, protectiveness or control and punitiveness, which will be detailed in Chapter 5.

Family roles

Though there is little emphasis in the literature on the effect of the roles played by specific family members on adolescent adjustment, it seemed theoretically important given the aim of investigating the way in which families affect children's behaviour. Most research on allocation of family roles pertains to the division of labour between parents. Decades ago, thinking about this matter was strongly influenced by Parsons and Bales' (1955) theory of a sex division between instrumental and expressive roles, the former (income provision and decision-making) being predominantly masculine and the latter (contribution to members' emotional wellbeing) being predominantly feminine. More recent efforts (e.g. Crosby, 1987) have assumed a negotiation of task allocations between spouses, but empirical studies still report females performing the bulk of tasks concerned with childcare and household maintenance (Allan, 1985; Broman, 1988; Haas, 1981; Hardesty and Bokemeier, 1989).

The relation between family size and participation by the husband is apparently negative, contrary to expectations (Haas, 1981; Hardesty and Bokemeier, 1989) — a relationship that is attributed by Rexroat and Shehan (1987) to the husband's preoccupation with employment during the middle years of marriage. Finally, participation of children in the performance of family duties may result from an absence of adults, from poverty, or from a deliberate attempt by parents to teach responsibility and sharing. Unfortunately, there are few substantial findings concerning these determinants and consequences of children's participation in family activities. McPartland and Epstein (1975) found students who were involved in family decision-making were more apt to be self-reliant and more satisfied with school. Griswold (1980) reported a small but significant correlation between family activities (especially going to the library) and maths, vocabulary and reading achievement in all races.

Our measures of family roles, specifically the sex and generation of the maintenance and status role performer and sex and age differentiation and concentration of family roles in general, irrespective of content will be introduced, along with parental practices, in Chapter 6 after a detailed description in Chapter 5.

Peer relations

In considering the relevance of friends for the focal subject's adjustment, one faces a dilemma of causal explanation. Do friends' attitudes and behaviour affect the focal subject, or does the focal subject select friends with beliefs and actions similar to the self? As our study was not longitudinal, there is no way to answer this question with our data. Other studies, however, strongly suggest the primacy of selection, rather than the influences of interactive processes, in bringing about self—friend similarity. In Newcomb's 1961 longitudinal study of friendship patterns in living accommodations for university students, similarity in pretest values of friendship pairs obtained from nominations later in the period studied were greater than the similarity for pretest values based on pairs defined from friendship nominations obtained early in the acquaintance process, when they presumably knew less about each other's values. Epstein's (1989) data show that current friends of ninth-graders were more similar to the focal subjects on several academic and non-academic measures than their friends had been in sixth and seventh grade. Scott (1965) found very little evidence of distinctive influence on university students' values from co-residents in group living houses, but rather significant selection effects: New students tended to join groups whose members had values similar to their own. We will, therefore, assume, for this study that any similarities between focal subjects and their friends are due to selection rather than to influence processes, and reflect the saliency of that variable.

Epstein (1989) has distinguished three bases for selection of friends by children. They would seem to apply to adults as well. The first basis is simple physical proximity: children are most apt to choose others with whom they are thrown together in the administrative or physical structure of the school. This is paralleled by Festinger, Schachter and Back's (1963) study of university student housing, where friendship patterns in a residential community developed along lines of the dwelling layout, with adjacent neighbours being more likely to choose one another than distant neighbours.

The next developmental basis for friendship acquisition, according to Epstein, is superficial similarity in age, sex and other obvious demographic characteristics. Only after considerable contact do more profound similarities come into play as determinants of friend selection—similarities in interests and attitudes. Kandel and Lesser (1972), for example, found parents and their children to have more similar values than did these adolescents and their friends, and Berndt, Miller and Park (1989) found that their junior high school students reported less influence from their peers than from their parents. Berndt (1989) assessed 297 seventh- and eighth-graders at the beginning and end of the school year. Among friends, there were increases in the similarity of school adjustment scores, both self-report and teacher-assessed, over the year, but not for grades. There the direction of movement was toward higher grades for students nominating friends with high grades, and increases in the school adjustment areas. It therefore seemed important to our study to include both similarity and strength in the variables representing the friends of our adolescents.

Cultural contributions

Cross-cultural research emanated from studies of national character, which were originated by psychological anthropologists (e.g. Kardiner, 1945). The early days saw culture mainly represented by anecdotal character studies based on interviews with selected representatives of the culture or group, such as Thomas and Znaniecki's *The Polish Peasant in Europe and America* (1958), Mead's *Coming of Age in Samoa* (1943), and Benedict's *The Chrysanthemum and the Sword* (1946). In 1938, Murdock established the Human Relations Area Files, in 1953 Whiting and Child's book *Child Training and Personality* was published, and in Segall's (1979) book, we saw the emergence of culture as a variable in research.

More recently, cross-cultural studies of work relations by Hofstede (1980) led to a classification on individual and collective values of various cultures. Triandis *et al.* (in their summaries of many studies in the six-volume *Handbook of Cross-Cultural Psychology*, 1980) report using etic (within-culture) and eco-logical (between-culture) analyses in comparing samples across cultures. Ideally, one can only interpret the differential contributions of cultures in relationships if the samples are equivalent, there is an appropriate range of representative cul-tures on the between-cultures variables, the measures are equivalent between cultures, and confounding cross-cultural variables can be partialled out statistic-ally. Shweder (1973) pointed out that there is no empirical relationship between within-culture and mean between-cultural findings. Though, as Leung and Bond (1989) and Hofstede (1980) have pointed out, it is statistically possible to find examples of non-parallel results, only when replication of theoretically sound within-culture relations are found in cross-cultural comparisons are cultural dif-ferences interpretable. We will elaborate on our approach to this problem when we develop our model in the next chapter.

Smith and Bond (1993) emphasize the importance of including cultural vari-ables, which they defined as an organized system of sharing meaning, to further enhance interpretation of cross-cultural data. In Chapter 8 we enter into our model the effect of the child's cultural environment. These cultural variables rep-resent the variance unaccounted for by the predictors replicated in all seven sam-ples, and are summarized in two forms: the mean of variables on which the samples differed and the dummy variables representing the samples and which were used to discount the contribution of culture when establishing the models in the earlier stages.

Summary

The model in Figure 1.1 outlines our study of adolescent adjustment as repli-cated across the seven cultures. It presents demographic and environmental antecedents of three subjective and objective domains of adjustment, whose effects are mediated by the coping styles of these adolescents. This model is based on the work of many scholars from many cultures. By integrating their variables into one study with more than one sample and more than one data source, we point the way to profitable areas of research as social scientists refine universal models to predict individual behaviour and interpret cultural differ-ences. The next chapter describes the samples, data collection and scale con-struction in more detail.

2

The Study

Following a pilot study in Brisbane (see Scott, Scott and McCabe, 1991), data for this study were collected in seven communities, located in seven cities — Berlin, Canberra, Hong Kong, Osaka, Phoenix, Taipei and Winnipeg — but were by no means representative of their countries. All samples came from urban areas with participation dependent upon the assent of school superintendents, principals, teachers, (sometimes) parents, and students; thus, the samples could not be considered random. The scope of the study was less broad than originally envisaged as initial contacts in some communities were aborted because of delay in administrative arrangements or because school administrators were unwilling to risk possible offence to parents or teachers, due to the subject matter of the study (family relations) or to the imposition on teachers' time.

All data were collected directly by the principal investigators (Canberra, Phoenix, Winnipeg) or by collaborators under the general guidance of the principal investigators (Dr Klaus Boehnke in Berlin, Dr Kwok Leung in Hong Kong, Professor Masamichi Sasaki in Osaka, the late Dr Shall-Way Cheng in Taipei). Selection of these communities depended on the contacts of collaborators in the several countries. Schools were generally chosen on the basis of their proximity to universities and the willingness of school officials to participate. These arrangements usually took several months of prior communications by mail, telephone, and visits to the schools, with procedures for obtaining consent of the participants followed in accordance with local practice (in two communities there were University Ethics Committees to be satisfied; in three communities the school principals' assent to participate was sufficient).

Questionnaires and Procedures

Student participants were solicited directly by the investigators or the teachers, and the questionnaires[1] were administered during class-time under the

---

[1] Instruments (in Cantonese, English, German, Japanese and Mandarin), culture specific statistics and raw data used in this study may be obtained from the Social Science Data Archives, The Australian National University, Canberra, A. C. T. 0200, Australia, citing W. A. Scott and R. Scott's Cross-Cultural Study Number B0529.

supervision of an investigator, a research assistant (in Taipei) or a teacher (Berlin, Hong Kong and Osaka). In Berlin, Osaka, and some Phoenix schools, this step followed initial approval of parents. Completion of the 14-page questionnaire required about 35 minutes, with the resulting numbers of questionnaires shown in Table 2.1. There was an excess of female over male students in five of the communities, generally reflecting the composition of the classes contacted there (e.g., psychology and social science in Canberra and Phoenix).

A nine-page questionnaire for parents was sent home with students, accompanied by a letter from the investigator explaining the purpose of the study and requesting that one parent (not specified which) fill it out and return it in the sealed envelope provided—either via the student to the school (in Berlin, Hong Kong, Osaka and Taipei) or by mail to the principal investigator (in Canberra, Phoenix and Winnipeg). Altogether, 67% of the children had responding parents. The lowest percentage (25%) was in Hong Kong, where only one in four parents (randomly selected) was asked to participate. Elsewhere, a questionnaire was sent to all parents, and the overall proportion replying was 77%, with the highest percentage of respondents (94%) in Taipei and the lowest (52%) in Berlin. In 63% of the cases the responding parent (or guardian) was female, and this proportion varied from 33% in Taipei to 83% in Phoenix.

After administration of the students' questionnaires, their teacher was asked to describe each participating student separately according to the instructions on the statements provided on the three-page questionnaire. These were collected a few days later by the investigator. At least one teacher's report was available for 83% of the students. The lowest percentage (36%) was in Hong Kong, where only those students with a parent responding plus one in every four students with no responding parent was represented in these measures (again, as with the parent sample, randomly selected). Some students in Berlin, Hong Kong and Winnipeg were rated by more than one teacher, in which case the mean teachers' rating was used for data.

Scale Development

A comparison of cultures is fraught with ambiguities of interpretation. It is easy enough to establish that samples from two or more cultures are significantly different in mean scores on a particular variable, but it is far from easy to establish the basis for any such differences that emerge. A difference may, indeed, be due to some hypothesized underlying determinant—for instance, a difference in mean hostility of children may be due to a cultural difference in parental punitiveness. On the other hand, the difference may be due to artefacts of measurement, for example, errors (or subtle differences) in translation, differences in the populations sampled, or differences in response styles of subjects in the various cultures, as discussed by Leung and Bond in their 1989 paper.

TABLE 2.1 *Sample sizes*

Community	Number of questionnaires from:			Schools	Number of Teachers	Classes	% Male	% in Grade:					
	Students	Parents	Teachers					7	8	9	10	11	12
Hong Kong	498	123[a]	180[a]	1	29	15	46	0	0	29	31	31	9
Taipei	535	504	533	5	14	20	50	27	21	0	22	33	0
Osaka	355	298	355	3	8	8	38	12	12	11	25	13	27
Berlin	247	129	222	8[b]	10	12	57	22	3	14	34	19	7
Winnipeg	111	82	110	5	18	18	38	29	20	14	9	15	13
Phoenix	399	276	394	6	37	37	27	0	0	29	22	28	22
Canberra	386	274	315	2[b]	9	11	39	9	11	17	23	17	24
TOTAL	2531	1686	2109	30	125	121	42	14	10	16	24	22	15

[a] Parent and teacher questionnaires were solicited only for a random sample of students.
[b] In addition to these students, selected in classes, other students from around the city were selected individually.

Translation-induced differences might occur, for example, when a rating scale with categories "very much," "quite a bit," "not very much," and "not at all" is translated into Japanese as "hijo-ni", "kanari," "sahodo . . . de nai," and "chitto-mo . . . de nai." Although the words may be the closest equivalents available, they do not necessarily fall on the same scale points of intensity in the two languages, so a mean rating difference between a Japanese and an English sample may reflect merely the differences in scale values of the words chosen. It is very hard to detect such subtle differences in word meanings, and users of either language may differ in extremity of meaning attached to each adverb.

It is partly because users of a given language differ in such subtle gradations of meaning that we cannot place too much emphasis on precise points of measurement implied by single words. Almost no one uses a language with the precision implied by lexicographers, and it is likely that intra-cultural differences are every bit as great as inter-cultural differences in word meanings. See Dunnigan, McNall and Mortimer (1993), for a more detailed discussion of metaphorical nonequivalence across cultures. Entire cultures may differ in modal response styles, such as acquiescence and extremity. Unless scales are counterbalanced to accommodate such styles, a cultural difference in scale scores may result simply from respondents in one sample acquiescing, or giving neutral responses, more frequently than in the other.

It is very difficult to overcome such methodological defects. Forward- and back-translation will not necessarily pick up subtle differences in scale location of items, for the Japanese "hijo-ni" is generally translated as "very," regardless of who is doing the translation. The best insurance against response-set differences across cultures is to vary the item format and to counterbalance all items of similar format in the original version.

An equally serious source of apparent cultural differences in mean scores is differences in the sampling procedures by which the groups were chosen. In comparing cultures it is very unusual to draw a probability sample of each from which to infer population differences. More commonly, a convenient sample is chosen in each, and what is convenient in one culture is not the same for all. If introductory psychology students serve as subjects, one must recognize that the class composition in Ryad, Saudi Arabia, is likely to be rather different from that in Des Moines, Iowa—in social status, exposure to news media, and other ways that might affect the dependent variables. Ideal sampling frames are often impossible to utilize, because some subjects or their gatekeepers are unwilling to cooperate.

Homogeneity

Measures of variables for this study were constructed both from the instruments of previous investigators and uniquely for this study (see the Appendix). They were translated into Cantonese, German, Japanese, and Mandarin, with adequacy of the translations subsequently checked by the collaborators and by item analyses.

In order to make sure that the intended variable distinguishes the cultures similarly in all of its manifestations (items), one may correlate all pairs of mean item scores, the homogeneity ratio (Scott, 1960), over the seven samples. Table 2.2 shows these data for the major scales containing more than one item along with the correlations among our three sources: child, parent and teacher. For instance, satisfaction with school has six items. The average inter-correlation of mean item scores over the seven samples is .77. This indicates that the six items distinguished the seven cultures in somewhat the same way, but by no means identically. These multi-item scales represent 10 of the 12 dependent variables, the personality scales, and family measures which were based on more than one item. All these data are based on the total combined sample. Mean intra-sample homogeneity ratios and inter-source correlations show similar results, though at a slightly lower level.

TABLE 2.2 *Common scale homogeneities and inter-source correlations*

Scale	$\underline{k}$	H.R.	$\underline{r}$ between	
			C^a and:	P and:
Satisfaction with school (C)	6	.77		
Academic performance (C)	2	.97		
Academic performance (P)	4	.90	.46	
Academic performance (T)	3	.74	.36	.41
Satisfaction with friends (C)	3	.44		
Interpersonal comfort (C)	6	.81		
Interpersonal competence (T)	7	.41	.29	
Satisfaction with family (C)	5	.90		
Satisfaction with family (P)	8	.98	.37	
Satisfaction with C's behaviour (P)	3	.72		
Self-esteem (C)	4	.89		
Self-esteem (T)	6	.89	.26	
Anxiety (C)	11	.33		
Anxiety (P)	5	−.03	.17	
Anxiety (T)	5	.56	.14	.04
Hostility (C)	2	.46		
Hostility (P)	12	.02	.11	
Hostility (T)	10	.79	.13	.24
Parental nurturance (C)	16	.97		
Parental nurturance (P)	4	.73	.00	
Parental protectiveness (C)	8	.57		
Parental protectiveness (P)	5	.93	.30	
Parental punitiveness (C)	5	.59		
Parental punitiveness (P)	4	.54	.40	

$\underline{k}$ = number of items; H. R. = average intercorrelation among item means.
[a] Sources: C = Child's report; P = Parents' report; T = Teacher's report.

Overall, the mean homogeneity ratio—that is, the mean scale inter-correlation among item means over the seven cultures—was .66. The highest mean item agreements for our cultures occurred for the child's self-reported and parent-judged academic performance, child's and parent's satisfaction with family, child-reported parental nurturance, and parent-reported protectiveness (all .90 or higher). For these scales, one can be reasonably certain that several measures of the variable yielded similar relative scores for the seven cultures; that is, the cross-cultural differences are reliable. The lowest homogeneity ratios appear for the scales of anxiety, hostility, teacher-judged interpersonal competence, and the child's satisfaction with friends, which implies that the cross-cultural comparisons are suspect, for different ways of measuring the variables did not yield the same results.

Generally, our scales include all a priori items which show average inter-item correlations (r_{it}) of at least .10 and also mean inter-item correlations inside the scale of at least .05 higher than their mean correlation with the items of any other scale, to ensure convergent and discriminant validity of items for each scale within every sample (Campbell and Fiske, 1959). Items that met these two criteria in all samples were identified as part of the "common scale". In the relatively rare instance when no common set of homogeneous items could be found (with item-total correlations at least .10 in all samples), the a priori set of items was retained to represent the intended variable. The scale items resulting from these analyses are shown in the Appendix[2].

Reliability

Reliabilities were quite similar from one sample to another, indicating that the variables were measured with similar appropriateness in all cultures. The mean reliability of scales measuring our 10 major dependent variables was .66. Maximum reliabilities, averaging in the .80s, occurred for teachers' ratings of academic performance and parents' reports of their family satisfaction, while minimum reliabilities, averaging under .50, occurred for students' self-reports of their academic performance and parents' appraisals of their children's home behaviour. These differences are, in part, attributable to scale lengths and degree of similarity of item wording, both of which tend to increase scale reliabilities. Although far from satisfactory as instruments for individual diagnosis, the scales of them are suitable for correlational analyses within large groups.

Validity

As reliability estimates from coefficient alpha (Cronbach, 1951) are substantially *inflated* by halo effects, they do not necessarily offer good evidence of scale

---

[2] For sample specific information on any data presented in the book, contact the Social Science Data Archives at the address given in the footnote on p. 21.

validity. Agreement among independent sources concerning a common variable is often used as an indicator of validity. The levels of inter-source agreement on variables listed in Table 2.2 ranged from a correlation of zero between children and parents' ratings of parental nurturance to .46 for children and parents' judgement of academic performance. These mean inter-source agreement (.26 for child—parent, .24 for child—teacher and .23 for parent—teacher) are very similar to those reported by Achenbach, McConaughy and Howell (1987; .25, .20 and .27, respectively). This emphasizes the fact that cross-source data are dependent on unique knowledge or differing perspectives (and, of course, by the effect of different item selection or wording). This highlights the issue of whether or not one can use other judgments of behaviour as a validation of self-report. We will be demonstrating this in forthcoming chapters when we show that the predictors of the child's level of adaptation are not always the same when described by parent or teachers or child. However, before we present some summarizing data on the differential effects of using the same versus cross-source data when predicting adjustment, we will first briefly summarize the method used to calculate our descriptive data.

Scale Intercorrelations

The data collected for this study are conceptualized as falling into the categories presented in Figure 1.1 in Chapter 1, the outcome or dependent variables, the mediating or intervening variables and the antecedent or independent variables. Before introducing their content we will review the general analysis framework used in the analyses reported here.

The search for interrelations among variables was performed within each sample separately, using the culture-specific scales (assuming these were the most valid measures), and the mean correlation was computed over the seven samples. The significance of the mean correlation was tested in one of two ways—by a t-test of the mean r (converted from Fisher's z-transformation) in ratio to the standard error of rs over the seven samples, and by means of Fisher's (1941) *Chi-square* test of results from several independent samples. The former test is simpler to compute and treats all samples as equally weighted, while the latter test weights samples in proportion to their sizes. Equal weighting seemed more appropriate, because the sample size obtained was, in large part, arbitrary, and we saw little reason to weight Taipei, for example, more heavily than Winnipeg in estimating an average effect over all samples. In any case, inferences from the two tests were nearly identical in all marginal cases where both were applied.

Source effects

The desirability of obtaining data from more than one source when developing models to predict behaviour is indisputable. If a child reported both satisfaction with family and self-esteem, the two measures could be highly confounded, due to a pervasiveness in the responses of the child either toward "pollyannaism" (Boucher and Osgood, 1969; Scott and Peterson, 1975) or toward "plaintive set" (Henderson, Byrne and Duncan-Jones, 1981). A similar confounding might occur for measures of punitiveness and the child's hostility both obtained from the parent. Similarity of results across source, as across samples, is a refreshing confirmation of findings; a lack of replication leaves one to ponder whether it is in the eyes of the beholder (the source), the differential behaviours sampled in different situations, or in the methodology.

To give some idea of the extent of source effects in the present analyses, Table 2.3 also shows Multiple-R^2s obtained when predictors came from the same source as the outcome, compared with those obtained when the predictors and outcome came from different sources. (Variables unique to one source, such as age, sex and attitudes of course contribute to both same- and cross-source differences.) On average, the cross-source R^2s are less than half the size of the same-source R^2s for the 12 measures of adjustment. The biggest change is in predicting the child's satisfaction with family from the parent's or teacher's assessment of other variables rather than the child's.

TABLE 2.3 *Multiple-R^2s from same- and cross-source predictors*

Outcome	Model[a]	Same-source	Cross-source
Adjustment measures			
School satisfaction (C)[b]	.23	.26	.16
Academic performance (C)	.23	.23	.23
Academic performance (P)	.26	.26	.16
Academic performance (T)	.48	.48	.18
Satisfaction with friends (C)	.22	.22	.09
Interpersonal competence (C)	.30	.30	.11
Interpersonal competence (T)	.35	.35	.02
No. of friends chosen (C)	.10	.10	.10
Sociometric status (F)	.06	.06	.06
Family satisfaction (C)	.43	.43	.00
Family satisfaction (P)	.23	.20	.10
Satisfaction with child (P)	.21	.27	.09
Mean R^2	.26	.26	*.11*
Mediators			
Self-esteem (C)	.10	.10	.01
Self-esteem (T)	.08	.08	.02
Anxiety (C)	.09	.09	.00
Hostility (P)	.22	.22	.08
Hostility (T)	.14	.14	.05
School means study (C)	.22	.22	.22
Mean R^2	*.14*	*.14*	*.06*

[a] With cultural differences partialled out (see Chapter 7).
[b] Sources: C = Child; P = Parent; T = Teacher; F = Friends.

However, this comparison does not completely answer the question of relative validities of using same- and cross-source predictors, as the use of cross-source measures probably over-corrects for source bias, just as same-source measures tend to exaggerate it. Similar behaviour is responded to differently when judging someone else than when reporting on actions based on one's introspection as the judges are calling on different referent groups, based on their own unique experiences, when making their ratings. For instance, in the present study, the students themselves, their parents and their teachers were all asked to judge the academic performance of the student. While the student may be compared to others in the class when the teacher is making the judgment, the parent may be comparing the child to his/her own performance at that age. In contrast, the child may be using an imaginary ideal when evaluating her/his own performance.

To replicate content, wording has to vary depending on whether the respondent is introspecting or judging others. In our study, the scale items often were not identical in order to try to focus the respondent's mind on a similar, underlying concept, or latent trait. This is particularly true in the realm of family relations where differing perspectives of the family members preclude identification of a single characteristic similarly recognized by all. And, certainly, when one gets into the area of our mediating variables, there is a real question as to whether or not variables such as self-esteem or hostility, as seen through others' eyes, are the same variable as those reported by the individual about oneself. Nevertheless, cross-source correlations tend to be smaller than same-source correlations, one should nevertheless require that they be significantly different from zero.

Summary

Changing the source of the predictors from the same or a different source in comparison to the adjustment measure did lower the variance accounted for by half, on average, though there was some variability in that. Whether this is because of the control of the halo effect or whether it merely is substituting a less knowledgeable cross-source for one which more accurately reflects the real antecedents of the adjustment state, is open to debate. In general, family patterns are associated with children's personality characteristics in the expected ways. However, it should be kept in mind that:

- These relationships are at very modest levels when possibilities for same-source contamination are precluded.
- Low cross-source correlations probably resulted because of lack of range in the scales as deviant families are less likely to participate.
- Family descriptions from parents cover whole family relations which may vary by child, whereas the specific adjustment of the child participating in the study could be markedly different from the average in the family.

- Personality is related not to "reality" but to the perception of the judge: self or role partner.

Sampling effects

Obviously, how subjects are recruited for a study can affect results. We first should reiterate the ways in which the seven samples were alike. All our subjects were adolescents, enrolled in secondary schools in industrialized Occidental and Oriental societies. Furthermore, they were most likely from literate families.

There were two major differences in the samples that could have contributed to sample differences, availability of marks and participation by parents. No marks were available for Hong Kong and Osaka subjects or for some children in other samples. Only Taipei and Winnipeg had grades for all (with one missing mark an exception). To ascertain whether or not the overall structure of the models for predicting adjustment would change, the combined samples for subjects with and without grades was run for all the adjustment measures. No differences affecting predictors with *betas* > .10 were found. Further, though children and/or parents from families with problems might be hypothesized as being less likely to participate, antecedent and mediators for outcomes based on comparing subjects with no parents to those with parents did not result in different versions of the final models.

These samples did have different means on some variables used in this study. We will deal with these in Chapter 8 as indicators of the social environment, represented by measured (cultural norms) and unmeasured (error) attributable to between sample differences. We cover the possible moderating effects of sex and age in some detail in Chapter 3 which we found to be negligible when taken into account along with our other variables. Though we do not discuss the possible moderating effect of minority group membership within samples, we did examine it, as we had found that it did moderate our data from Australia in a previous study (Scott and Scott, 1989), with migrants more likely to be less satisfied with school when doing well as far as marks were concerned though the native-born Australians showed a positive association between these two variables. Once again, though there was the association between migrant status and school means study, it was insignificant when other variables were taken into account and the effect of culture was partialled out.

The Role of the Mediator Variables

We hypothesize that the effect of antecedent variables on outcome is mediated by the coping styles of the individuals. An example will illustrate the mediating effect of parental nurturance on the relationship between family size and children's satisfaction with their family. Suppose the correlation between family size and satisfaction (r_{ab}) is –.10; the correlation between nurturance and satisfaction (r_{cb}) is .40, and the correlation between family size and nurturance (r_{ac}) is –.25. It is reasonable to hypothesize that the relation between family size and satisfaction is due to the low level of nurturance in large families. To test this mediating effect, one computes the partial correlation between family size and satisfaction, with nurturance held constant:

$$r_{ab.c} = [r_{ab} - (r_{ac} * r_{bc})]/[(1 - r^2_{ac})(1 - r^2)]1/2$$
$$= [-.10 - (.40 * - .25)]/[(1 - .40^2)(1 - .25^2)]$$
$$= 0.00$$

In this example the relationship between family size and family satisfaction has been reduced to zero when the level of family nurturance is held constant. Usually, the amount of reduction is not so great, but the correlation may fall from a significant to a non-significant level, in which case the inference of mediation by the hypothesized variable (nurturance) is tentatively accepted. If, on the other hand, the correlation between family size and member satisfaction remains significant with nurturance partialled out, one must conclude that at least part of the effect of family size is direct, or mediated by some other (unmeasured) variable.

Analysis Procedures

All of these variations in sample selection, and the ultimate dependence on consent of the participants, mean that differences in results from one community to another could have come simply from differences in their samples of students, and we have no good way of knowing whether other samples from these same countries would have yielded similar results. The most dependable analyses, therefore, are those which replicate relationships over the several samples; the argument being that, if similar findings appeared in most of the communities studied, regardless of differences in sampling procedures, then the results may safely be regarded as dependable.

To lead the readers into the data, we will introduce each group of predictors separately, presenting their descriptive statistics first, followed by the effects they have on the source-specific adjustment ratings. Models diagramming the predictors of both the intervening or mediating coping styles and the outcome measures of adjustment are established using multiple repression analyses, as one of our main foci is to establish the relative contribution of predictors from variable domains or outcomes with different foci and reported on by different judges. Rather than using the hierarchical procedure as recommended by Baron and Kenny (1986), an analogous method was used which compares the zero order correlations and *beta* weights in standard multiple regressions where the category of variables has been specified by the theoretical model. As we are interested in the commonality of relationships across samples, the models are based on the mean sample statistics, which were approximated by using the predictor's *beta* weights from equations containing dummy variables representing the presence or absence of each of the samples. To avoid the effects of singularity, the variable for one of the samples (the one with the lowest correlations with the dependent or mediating variable) was removed.

The general procedure followed for each of the outcome and mediating variables separately was to select antecedents from the domain of variables under consideration whose mean zero-order correlations were significant ($p < .05$, 2-tail). Non-significant correlates were excluded from that and all further regression analyses because, at this stage in the model development, we were not concerned with moderating effects, i.e. those whose effects depend on the presence of another variable. Discussion of possible moderating or interactive effects from sex and age with coping styles will be taken up in the next chapter.

Using all the significant antecedents, a preliminary multiple-regression is performed which also includes the significant mediating variables and the dummy variables representing the extraneous sample differences. Those with significant *beta* weights $\geq .10$ are retained as predictors of that specific outcome variable along with the significant mediating variables. Solid arrows indicate the predicted relationships (antecedents to mediators and mediators to outcomes) whereas the dotted lines represent the direct effects of antecedents on the dependent variables, *not* predicted by us. To emphasize the contrast between the results of variables looked at in the context of other variables (the *beta* weights) versus alone, the bracketed zero-order correlations for all predictors follow the *beta* weights. As the shared variance of the association between two variables is calculated as the square of the product-moment r, so the shared variance between two variables in a multiple regression analysis is calculated as the product of the *beta* weight (the weight unique to that predictor when taken in the context of the other equation variables) and its zero-order correlation, r. In addition, variables with both direct and indirect effects are predictors whose zero-order correlations are lessened only partially. When included with other variables, they have both their direct and indirect relationships shaded in the figures.

After establishing the relevant antecedents from the demographic variables in Chapter 4, Chapter 5 sees us through selecting the relevant family relations variables for possible entry into the models in Chapter 6. The tables in Chapter 5 display the relationship of demographic characteristics to the family variables, pointing to their indirect contribution, through their effect on the family variables, to predictions of adjustment. The demographic measures whose *beta* weights now drop below .10, will now be removed from the model.

Chapter 7 sees the increase in the amount of variance accounted for by inclusion of peer similarity and strength variables along with the demographic and family variables which still contribute significantly to predicting adjustment. The final step is to examine the remaining unexplained variance, represented until then by the dummy variables which stand for the contribution from differing samples means or to unmeasured content. We are now ready for examination of the dependent and mediating variables in our study of adjustment of adolescents.

3

Measures of Adjustment and Their Personality and Demographic Correlates

Studies of adjustment are based on various typologies. Epstein and McPartland (1977b) treated as "outcome" variables sets of measures that we would classify both as "adjustment" and "personality." Among the "school coping skills" was an index, "quality of school life," which is very close to our "satisfaction with school." Their "prosocial school-task behaviour" seems similar to our "meaning of school." Their "disciplinary adjustment" is akin to our "hostility", which we have conceptualized as a style of coping or a personality variable. Their other "dependent variables"—anxiety, self-reliance, and self-esteem—also seem more properly, within our framework, to be considered as personality variables, rather than as measures of adjustment, for they have no specific foci, but would appear instead to be fairly general and stable properties of the child manifest in the face of various demands for adaptation.

Measures of Adjustment

Following our view that adjustment refers to specific environmental foci, here are adjustment measures for the three foci—academic, interpersonal, and family—each from two perspectives: subjective and objective. Items assigned to each scale are shown in the Appendix and illustrated in Table 3.1. In addition to the exact wording of all items, the source of each question is given in the Appendix when it did not originate with us. The items were designated a priori for each variable of interest, and the appropriateness of assignment judged by two criteria:

1. The mean (corrected) item-total correlation was at least .10 with the a priori scale and averaged no more than .05 less with outside items; and
2. The correlation between each pair of scales was at least .20 lower than their mean reliability.

This resulted in fairly homogeneous and relatively distinct scales. The advantage of this procedure over factor analysis for scale definition is that it preserves the variables of a priori interest and ignores trivial methodological differences due to item wording which might have generated uninteresting factors.

TABLE 3.1 *Adjustment scales and sample items*

Scale[a]	k[b]	alpha[c]	Sample item
Academic adjustment			
Satisfaction with school	6	.72	How satisfied are you with your school here?
Academic performance (C)	2—3	.54	How do you feel about your ability to do academic work?
Academic performance (P)	4	.68	How would you describe this child as a student?
Academic performance (T)	3—4	.80	How well does this student perform in classwork?
Interpersonal adjustment			
Satisfaction with friends (C)	3—4	.54	Are you happy with the sorts of friends you have here?
Interpersonal comfort (C)	6	.71	How easy is it for you to make new friends?
Interpersonal competence (T)	7	.82	How does he or she fit in the class socially?
Number of friends chosen	1	[d]	Of all the students *in this class* which ones would you most like to eat lunch go shopping or go to a movie with?
Sociometric status	1	[d]	(same)
Family adjustment			
Satisfaction with family (C)	5	.80	My home is a happy place to be.
Satisfaction with family (P)	8	.81	Are you happy with the sorts of friends your children have?
Satisfaction with child's behaviour (P)	3—6	.49	Cooperative.

[a]   Sources of measure: C = Child; P = Parent; T = Teacher.
[b]   k is number of items in culture-specific scale; varied from one sample to another.
[c]   Mean scale reliability estimates from Cronbach's (1951) alpha.
[d]   Single item; no estimate of reliability available.

Reliability

It is noteworthy that the results were quite constant over the seven samples, that is, the scales of adjustment had similar meanings in all cultures. The average standard deviation across-cultures of reliability coefficients for the ten multi-item scales in Table 3.1 was .05. This means that a reliable scale in one culture — such as teachers' ratings on the child's academic and interpersonal performance — was generally reliable in other cultures as well, while scales of low reliability — such as parent appraisals of the child's behaviour — tended to be so in all cultures. One source of high reliability in teachers' ratings is the constant item format, which was maintained to make the task easy for teachers.

Friendship patterns

Two measures of interpersonal adjustment were single item variables reflecting both the subjective and objective evaluation of peer interaction in the school class. Respondents were asked, "Of all students in this class, which ones would you most like to eat lunch or go shopping or go to a movie with? (Name as many as you wish, but write both first and last names for each person.)" Frequencies of nomination and proportions of nominations received by class members are shown in Table 3.2. These two statistics were used as measures of interpersonal adjustment, namely number of friends chosen and the sociometric status variable popularity for recreation. The number of friends nominated averaged around 2.6 over the seven samples, with the largest number in Osaka (3.75) and the fewest (1.87) in Hong Kong. Sociometric status or popularity was not a very reliable variable, largely because interpersonal preferences of this sort tend to be mutual rather than consensual within groups such as a classroom (Scott and Cohen, 1979a, 1978b). Perhaps a more discriminating instrument, such as ranking or rating of each class member, would have yielded more stable measures, but this procedure used on university students (Scott, 1965) also yielded mainly reciprocal, rather than consensual, choices of friends. Consensual choices are more likely to appear for objective attributes such as ability, rather than for affective attributes, such as liking. To avoid some of the instability of the measures, scores for children from classes with six or fewer raters were eliminated.

TABLE 3.2 *Choices for recreational companion*

	Hong Kong	Taipei	Osaka	Berlin	Winnipeg	Phoenix	Canberra
Number chosen by S							
Mean*	1.87[c]	2.12[c]	3.75[a]	3.31[b]	2.77[b]	2.19[c]	2.27[c]
S.D.	1.95	1.98	2.93	2.42	1.81	1.65	1.92
% of class who chose S							
Mean	.04	.06	.06	.11	.11	.07	.07
S.D.	.04	.07	.05	.11	.11	.08	.07
Number of Ss *in*							
classes > 6	498	535	355	215	70	357	217

*   z-scores with an identical superscript are not significantly different, at $p < .05$, by Newman-Keuls test.

Interrelationship

As spelled out in Chapter 1, a priori measures of adjustment to academic matters and interpersonal and family relations, the three salient areas of concern for adolescents, were developed using information provided by the child, a parent, teachers and fellow classmates. Table 3.3 illustrates the distinction among domains of adjustment empirically. Using mean within-sample statistics to avoid inflated correlations due to sample differences in the variable means, scale intercorrelations are shown in Table 3.3, along with the mean within-sample scale reliabilities (Cronbach's (1951) coefficient alpha) in parentheses on the diagonal. (See Table 2.1 for the number of student, parent and teacher respondents in each of the seven samples).

TABLE 3.3 *Mean within-sample correlations among measures of adjustment (culture-specific scales)*

	1	2	3	4	5	6	7	8	9	10	11	12
Academic adjustment												
1. Satisfaction with school	(.72)											
2. Self-appraised academic performance	.33*(.56)											
3. Parent-appraised academic performance	.27*	.34*(.68)										
4. Teacher-appraised academic performance	.15*	.36*	.39*(.80)									
Interpersonal adjustment												
5 Satisfaction with friends	.32*	.20*	.09*	.09*(.54)								
6. Self-reported interpersonal comfort	.17*	.20*	.04	.02	.42*(.71)							
7. Teacher-judged interpersonal competence	.11*	.14*	.07	.28*	.16*	.28*(.82)						
8. Number of friends chosen	.12*	.09*	.07*	.08*	.23*	.18*	.16* a					
9. Sociometric status	.06	.06*	.11*	.12*	.07*	.42*	.11*	.24* a				
Family adjustment												
10. Satisfaction with family	.27*	.16*	.12*	.03	.24*	.18*	.05*	.11*	.06*(.80)			
11. Parental satisfaction with family	.08*	.05*	*.31**	.08*	.07*	.07*	.06*	.04	.08*	.32*(.81)		
12. Parents' satisfaction with child's behaviour	.15*	.15*	*.35**	.20*	.17*	.17*	.13*	.08*	.08*	.19*	.28*(.49)	

* p < .05. (Error variance of mean product-moment r estimated from standard deviation of rs over seven samples). Minimum sub-sample n = 57.
Note: Diagonal figures in parentheses are mean scale reliabilities estimated from Cronbach's (1951) coefficient alpha. Underlined rs are within the same domain, r*s in italics are same source, cross-domain*:
a Single item; alpha could not be computed.

The mean within-domain intercorrelation for these subjective and objective measures of adjustment scales are .31, .23, and .26 respectively (underlined in Table 3.3), while the mean between-domain correlations are all lower: for academic (mean r = .14), friend (mean r = .12), and family (mean r = .13). That is, the measures of adjustment within a given domain tend to show more agreement than do measures between domains.

Nevertheless, there is some degree of commonality across domains, as shown by the mean cross-domain correlation of .13: good adjustment in one domain tends to be accompanied by good adjustment in the other two domains. Part of this commonality is due to source effects: for instance, self-report measures tend to be substantially intercorrelated, as do teachers' ratings across domains. The mean correlation over the 19 variables when taken from the same source is .23, as contrasted to an average cross-domain correlation of .09 when measures from a common source are ignored (rs in italics). This indicates that there is a small tendency for adjustment in one domain to correspond to adjustment in other domains irrespective of source of information. Academic, interpersonal, and family adjustment are distinct, though correlated for these adolescents. There was a mean r of .34 between corresponding adjustment scores from children, parents, and teachers, when averaged over the seven samples. Even so, their distinctiveness seems more salient than their overlap. We will come back to this when we discuss the differential effects of personality on adjustment.

Table 3.3 is based on data from all respondents to the relevant measures. Obviously, children without responding parents are, by definition, omitted from the correlations in rows 3, 11, and 12, whose data came from parents. Separate analyses were performed on the 1686 children with parents responding. The results were nearly identical to those reported in Table 3.3, which suggests that missing parents' replies did not bias the results of interest here.

Validity

It is not easy to ascertain validity, the relationship of our scales to "true facts" of adaptive success. Within a domain, measures were substantially intercorrelated, providing some evidence for construct validity. Across domains there were moderate (though smaller) intercorrelations indicating that the child's adjustment to school, friends and family tended to be consistent, although the relationships were not large when source effects were eliminated by considering only cross-source correlations. In the domain of academic achievement, three sources of measures were considered: child, parent and teacher. The last of these might reasonably be considered a criterion against which the other two sources could be validated. Teacher-judged academic performance was itself correlated, on average, .58 with children's average marks shown in school records from the five samples for whom they were made available. Using teacher ratings as criteria, the child's self-rated academic performance correlated, on average, .36 and parent-judged academic performance .39 with the criterion. These are among the highest correlations in Table 3.3.

Validity of adjustment measures for the other two domains is a bit more difficult to establish. Nevertheless, the child's self-rating on interpersonal comfort correlated .28 with teachers' judgments on this variable, while the child's satisfaction with his/her family was correlated .32 with his/her parents' reciprocated family satisfaction. These correlations, while not high, are within the range ordinarily encountered for validity coefficients based on measures from different sources (Achenbach, McConaughy and Howell, 1987) and will be discussed again when we review source and sampling effects.

Coping Styles: Personality and School Means Study

As our personality and orientation traits can be defined as representations of the ability to cope or adjust to specific environmental demands, we will look briefly at those relationships now. The variables included in our study are:

self-esteem (child- and teacher-rated);
anxiety (child-, parent- and teacher-rated);

hostility (child-, parent- and teacher-rated);
school means study (parent- and child-rated only).

Table 3.4 presents a brief description of these variables, along with data on their reliabilities (see Appendix for the complete scales used in this study).

TABLE 3.4 *Personality and school means study scales and sample items*

Scale	$\underline{k}$[a]	alpha[b]	Sample item
Self-esteem			
Child's self-report	4	.67	How do you feel about yourself?
Teacher's report	6	.81	Is self-confident.
Anxiety			
Child's self-report	16—19	.73	I shrink from facing a crisis or difficulty.
Parents' report	6—8	.58	Afraid of new things.
Teacher's report	5—6	.64	Worries about many things.
Hostility			
Child's self-report	2—3	.39	At times I feel like smashing things.
Parents' report	12	.76	This child is often rebellious and disobedient.
Teacher's report	10	.87	Talks back to the teacher.
School means study			
Child's self-report	4—6	.59	Which of the following things are most important to you in school? (studying)
Parents' report	6—7	.56	From your point of view, which of the following things should be most important to your child at school? Trying to get good marks.

[a] $\underline{k}$ is number of items in culture-specific scale; varied from one sample to another.
[b] Mean scale reliabilities estimated from Cronbach's (1951) coefficient alpha.

School means study

This scale was constructed from a priori items representing the salience of studying, friends, recreation and discipline by teachers when children or parents think about the meanings of school. Besides a checklist containing these meanings of school, there was also an open-ended question requesting the respondent to describe the meaning of school in his/her own words. By far the most common meanings were studying and friends, with concern for recreation tending to go with emphasis on friends, while concern for discipline tended to go with emphasis on studies. These two sets of concerns tended to be antithetical, that is negatively correlated. We therefore constructed a difference variable, which was the difference between emphasis (in both the free-response and the rank-ordering measures) on studies or discipline and the emphasis on friends or recreation and labelled it "school means study" to depict the scoring direction.

Interrelationship

We were able to obtain measures of children's personalities from two or three sources. Though not so high in agreement as for adjustment measures, these correlations (Table 3.5) were all significant when averaged over the seven samples, and their mean was .15 (in contrast with the mean r of .34 between corresponding adjustment scores from children, parents and teachers). The discrepancy may be attributable to two sources: lower reliability of the personality measures and lower "visibility" of the inferred traits being assessed. The mean within-sample agreement between parent and child scores on school means study was not significant (r=.15). Obviously parents and children do not necessarily share the same views about the function of schools.

TABLE 3.5 *Agreement concerning children's personalities (mean product-moment r over seven samples)*

Trait	Child—Parent	Child—Teacher	Parent—Teacher
Self-esteem	[a]	.14*	[a]
Anxiety	.20*	.18*	.09*
Hostility	.11*	.14*	.20*

* $p < .05$ (error variance estimated over the seven sample rs). Minimum sub-sample n = 82.
[a] No measure available from parent.

Demographic Antecedents

In describing variables associated with adjustment in our opening chapter, considerable attention has been paid to demographic correlates. Our study included some, but by no means all, of them. For demographic data about the child, the sex and age variables are self-evident. The marks are the average of those obtained from school records, normed separately within each sample. These were missing for two samples, so ns for equations using this variable was necessarily reduced. Verbal ability was scored from the administration of the Taft and Bodi's (1980) Cloze Test, which required the child to fill in words (or characters) that were missing from a paragraph. Scoring (number of correct responses out of 10) was done by a native speaker in each sample.

The demographic characteristics of the parent refer to the respondent parent (self-determined). Again, sex and age are self-evident. Education was coded as the number of years completed, including tertiary level, which was specifically probed for.

Demographic characteristics of the family included the number of adults and the number of children coded from a list of family members obtained from both parents and children. There was very close agreement between parents' and children's reports on the number of children in the family (mean r over the seven samples = .89) but agreement on number of adults was generally not so high (mean r = .67). Presumably this resulted mainly from the presence of transient adults (adult siblings, grandparents) who were not similarly identified as family members by parents and children. Additional discrepancies may be due, in part, to the fact that parent-reported families constituted only a subset (67%) of the child-reported families as not all children had a parent also responding. The mean number of adults reported by children was 2.11 (S.D. = .20 over the seven samples), while the mean number of adults reported by parents was 2.10 (S.D. =.26). The mean number of children reported by students was 2.77 (S.D. = .50 over the seven samples), while the mean number of children reported by parents was 2.62 (S.D. = 0.53). Despite a correlation of only .67 between the child's and the parent's reports of the number of adults in the family, the pattern of correlates did not differ markedly, therefore, for simplicity's sake, only one source was used for both number of children and number of adults. The child's data were selected as there was less missing data.

Minority-group membership was defined as immigrant status of the child and its parents in Berlin, Canberra, Hong Kong, Taipei and Winnipeg, but not in Osaka and Phoenix, where there were no immigrants. In Phoenix, minority ethnic status—Black or Chicano—was used instead; this measure was based on judgment of the investigators (who were present at all testing sessions), confirmed by advice from the attending teacher. A three category code was constructed with 0 representing non-minority-group status, 1 standing for minority-group status for the parents only and 2 meaning that both child and parents belonged to a minority group.

Correlates of coping styles

Below is a brief description of the significant correlations between demographics and coping styles. These are based on the mean within sample rs, so the significant ones can be said to represent associations common to all samples. In the next chapters, those with significant influence on specific coping styles, determined by entering the significant variables into regression equations, along with dichotomies representing six of the seven cultures, will be presented as we develop our models of adolescent adjustment.

For self-reported self-esteem, the main predictors are with being young (.13), male (.15), getting good marks (.15), and having a relatively better educated responding parent (.08). Whereas, for teacher-judged self-esteem, marks (.23) and verbal ability (.13) along with an educated parent (.08) were the more important determinants. For the anxiety personality variable, being female was associated with high scores for both self-report and when judged by the teacher, whereas low marks correlated with self-reported and parent-judged high anxiety.

Turning to reports on the child's hostility, all three judges, the self, parent and teacher, showed a positive association between verbal ability and low hostility.

For both objective measures (parent and teacher-judged hostility), higher scores were associated with younger children (−.12 and −.11, respectively) and younger responding parent (−.08, −.10) plus lower marks (−.16, −.19), and verbal ability (−.09, −.14). Only for teachers, but, interestingly, not for parents, there was a strong association between being male and hostility (.22). And, finally, the school means study had a consistent cross-cultural association only with young age and low parental education.

Demographic and Coping Styles Correlates of Adjustment

In the following chapters we will be describing the *unique* contributions of the coping styles, demographic characteristics, and social environmental measures which hold across all samples. First, however, a description of our dependent variables as they relate to our demographic and coping style variables.

Academic adjustment

Demographic characteristics

The most consistent demographic correlate of academic adjustment was school marks, which had significant mean correlations with all three sources of information on academic performance (.41 children-rated, .45 parent-judged and .55 for teacher's reports) in the five samples where marks were available. In addition, marks correlated .19 with child's satisfaction with school. The child's verbal ability also correlated with all three measures of academic performance (.11, .15 and .27 for children, parent's and teacher's reports, respectively). And the responding parent's education was significantly associated with both the child's and the teacher's reports on academic performance (.08 and .17), but *not* with the parent's.

Age effects were inconsistent, being positively correlated with teachers' appraisals of academic performance(+.09) and negatively correlated with appraisals from the child (−.09). If this finding is dependable, it may suggest that students tend to become more self-critical with age, while their teachers are likely to find their academic performance improving as they mature.

While teachers tended to judge girls as more academically competent than boys (.13), this sex difference did not appear consistently for any of the other three measures of academic adjustment, including the child's satisfaction with school. Also family composition showed no important relation with any kind of adjustment. The number of parents in the family showed a mean product-moment correlation of .05 with parent-judged academic performance, while the number of children was negatively correlated, on average (mean r = −.05) with child-judged academic performance. Although statistically significant, these small correlations hardly sustain the belief among some teachers that single-parent families breed maladjustment in their children (e.g. Santrock and Tracy, 1978), or that only children tend to excel academically, for there is no association between number of adults in the family and academic performance.

Finally, it must be noted that the demographic variable family minority-group status showed no consistent relationships within the seven samples to the four outcomes measures of school adjustment. Only in Berlin was there a significant correlation between immigrant status and two of the outcomes: child's satisfaction with school and parent's judgment of the child's academic performance. That there was no consistent effect of minority-group membership on academic adjustment of high-school students was contrary to results previously obtained in several American studies with Blacks (Allen, 1988; Oliver, Rodriguez and Mickelson, 1985). It appears that in cross-national research, ethnic minority status cannot be treated as equivalent to Black American.

Coping styles

With the exception of the demographic characteristics, marks and verbal ability, both of which recognize innate intelligence, the greatest contributors to predicting academic adjustment are coping styles, with a strong source effect standing out. For example, self-esteem, reported by the child, was most highly related to child-reported academic adjustment (.41); it correlated .18 with parent and .10 with teacher-judged academic performance. Furthermore, teacher-judged self-esteem was most highly related to teacher-judged academic performance (.44) in comparison to .19 with the child's report and .13 with the parent's.

Next, parent-judged hostility was most related to parent-reported academic performance (−.38) in comparison to −.11 for children's report of academic performance and −.19 for teacher's, while teacher-judged hostility correlated −.38 with teacher-judged academic performance, −.11 with the child's and −.24 with the parent's judgment.

When examining the relationship between anxiety and academic adjustment, we find that child-reported anxiety was negatively correlated with all of these outcomes; −.16 with satisfaction with school, and −.30, −.10 and −.09 with the child's, parent's, and teacher's evaluation of performance.

Finally, the highest relationship to the child's report of school means study was with the child's own report of satisfaction with school (.31) and academic performance (.16), in comparison with a mean r of .12 with parent's report of academic performance, and a non-significant relationship to the teacher's evaluation.

In summary, superior academic performance tends to go along with the coping styles represented by high self-esteem, low anxiety and low hostility in the child and to attributing to school an academic rather than a social meaning. Though a large part of these relationships between academic adjustment and the child's personality and attitudinal characteristics may simply reflect a biased perspective of the source, the cross-source correlations were generally in the same directions, though of smaller magnitude, as the same-source correlations. In order of magnitude, to date the correlates of academic adjustment are: marks, self-esteem, hostility, anxiety, verbal ability; while demographic characteristics of children and parents do not account for much variance.

Interpersonal adjustment

It had originally been anticipated that the child's interpersonal adjustment would have a somewhat different pattern of correlates than academic adjustment—specifically, that sex and age would play a stronger role in the former relationships. This expectation was not generally confirmed. Only (female) sex proved to be a more important correlate of interpersonal than of academic adjustment, though the average relationship over the seven samples was not very high (.08 with satisfaction with friends, .05 with interpersonal comfort (self-report) and .09 with number of classmates chosen as friends by the child). The child's self-esteem and anxiety were both implicated in interpersonal adjustment in the same manner as in academic adjustment, and source effects were equally prominent.

Sociometric measures of interpersonal adjustment, though generally correlating with predictors in the same directions as the children's and teachers' reports, showed smaller magnitudes of association with only a significant positive correlation with teacher-judged self-esteem (.09) and a negative correlation with number of children in the child's family (−.07). Perhaps this is due to a ceiling effect in the sociometric measure: children typically did not name more than three or four classmates with whom they wanted to associate for recreation. Another sociometric item, "With whom would you like to study?", was very highly correlated with the sociometric measure "With whom would you like to recreate?", furthermore, it yielded the same pattern of correlates, so it has been deleted from any analyses presented here. In any event, both of the items used here were very crude sociometric measures of interpersonal adjustment.

Family adjustment

It was expected that family adjustment of the child would show a pattern of correlates similar to that for academic adjustment, but not interpersonal adjustment—under the assumption that peer-group relations function independently of family and school relations. The expected similarities with academic adjustment correlates generally emerged, but not the expected differences with interpersonal adjustment correlates. Overall, family adjustment was significantly correlated with the child's self-esteem, anxiety and hostility; younger children and children with better educated parents were more satisfied with their families; and parents were more satisfied with their child's behaviour if the child had good marks.

Potential Moderators

Before summarizing the more important findings of this chapter, the possible moderating effects on our models from such variables as age and sex need to be commented on. Overall the differences in relationship within sex and age were trivial; only 7% of age-predictor interactions and 6% of sex-predictor variable interactions were significant.

Gender differences

Though girls were significantly higher on all measures of adjustment except for both child and parent satisfaction with family, gender had a direct effect only on interpersonal adjustment, namely on satisfaction with friends and number of friends chosen. The effect of gender on child's satisfaction with school, friends and family, both child's and parent's rating on academic performance and child's report on interpersonal comfort and number of peers chosen, was mediated by the personality variable of self-esteem (higher for boys than for girls when reported by them), whereas the teacher's ratings of hostility (also higher for boys than for girls) mediated gender effects for satisfaction with school and the teacher's ratings on academic performance.

The consistent and strong relationship between maleness and self-esteem, in the composite sample with the effect of culture partialled out, is also significant within each culture, though it didn't reach significance at the 5% level (2-tail) for Berlin and Hong Kong. In addition to males reporting significantly higher self-esteem than girls, there is a further effect of gender on the child's report of self-esteem, whereas boys' report of self-esteem is unaffected by their own descriptions of overprotectiveness by their parents, girls' self-esteem is negatively affected. Interesting as this is, when we ran the regression equation on the combined sample with the sex-overprotection interaction included, the contribution was so low (*beta* < .05) that it was omitted in the models of adjustment.

Furthermore, except for overprotectiveness, predictors contribute similarly to the total variance when boys and girls are examined separately. Ohannessian, Lerner, Lerner and von Eye (1994) found similar gender concurrence in their study of family and emotional (our coping styles) adjustment. In our study, when the 12 adjustment models were compiled separately for boys and girls, the only significant differential effect of sex when all predictors were entered together, was for the child's family satisfaction, even though the boys and girls did not differ significantly on that measure of adjustment. However, this was due to the mediating effect of self-esteem, previously discussed. We conclude from this that the differential effects of gender on adolescent adjustment are not direct, but mediated by their differential relationship to coping styles measured in this study, self-esteem and hostility.

Age differences and similarities

Age does have a direct effect on some measures of adjustment. In addition, it has a indirect effect through its association with personality and the meaning of school. As with gender, the significant differential effect of age in our study was limited to 1 when entered into our developing models of adjustment; the age by self-esteem (teacher's report) interaction term significantly increased our ability to interpret and predict adjustment represented by the sociometric rating given to the child by his peers but this was accounted for by cultural differences in sociometric choices and has therefore been excluded from the model as it is impossible to specify what to attribute this to.

Though the child's self-report of self-esteem is negatively correlated with age ($r = -.22, p < .01$), the teacher's evaluation of self-esteem and age is uncorrelated ($r = .01$). Yet the interaction between age and self-esteem (teacher-reported) shows the older child with *lower* self-esteem predicting the sociometric status in addition to the younger child with high self-esteem. As both the teacher and peers are judging the child in the same behavioural milieu, it is surprising that these evaluations are dissimilar. Perhaps the teacher's evaluation of self-esteem are done within the framework of age-appropriate behaviour, a comparison less likely to be available to adolescents as they are of the same age cohort. Teachers expect older children to be more self-confident; though this is something that does not seem to be borne out by the child's self-report which shows younger children with higher scores, perhaps attributable to their stage in adolescent development and the stresses of maturation.

Summary

Overall, one can say that the three kinds of adjustment did not show markedly different correlates among the variables considered here. The important predictors can be summarized as follows:

1. Demographic characteristics of verbal ability and parent's education plus the meaning of school variable were associated, positively, only with academic adjustment.
2. Good academic, interpersonal and family adjustment were all associated with good marks and the mediating variables self-esteem (high) and anxiety (low).
3. Poor academic and family adjustment was associated with high scores on the coping-behaviour scale representing hostility.

4.   Older adolescents recorded lower scores on three mediating variables which represented the adjustment coping styles self-esteem, hostility and school-means-study scores.

5.   Older adolescents also scored lower on subjective measures of adjustment in contrast to teacher-judged high academic performance, which showed the teacher reporting older rather than younger children performing better.

It is noteworthy that, contrary to the reviewed studies, none of the other demographic variables measured in this study (minority-group status, family composition, age and sex of responding parent) were significantly related to any of the adjustment or personality (coping) measures (mean within-sample correlations).

In the following chapter we shall put these relationships into some simple models which will enable us to examine their effects in the context of other variables. To date we have only looked at predictors of adjustment as if they existed in a vacuum, not a condition found in the real world. We now take the first step and establish the coping style predictors of our adjustment or outcome variables, plus the demographic predictors of our mediating variables, themselves.

4

Models of Adjustment: Demographic Antecedents and Personality Mediators

Building on the assumption that individual characteristics, classified here as demographic variables, affect adjustment by their influence on coping behaviour, as represented by a person's personality and general orientation, we will now start developing our models of student adjustment to specific situations, as seen through their own eyes and through the eyes of others. The effects of the social situations in which our children operate, such as the family, the friendship network, and the general cultural milieu will be covered in succeeding chapters. Here we will be concerned with the effects of demographic characteristics on adjustment as mediated by the personality and meaning of school attributes. Using the overall strategy spelled out in Chapter 2, regression equations for outcome measures and the coping style mediators were developed by regressing each on their specific significant demographic antecedents, defined as those with significant zero-order correlations. If an antecedent had both a direct and an indirect (mediated) effect on the outcome variable, that is, contributed significantly, with a *beta* weight $\geq .10$, to both scores, the measure and its *beta* are shaded in the diagram for both. Models in this book are based on the total sample (minimum $n = 1686$, see Table 2.1) with the effects of culture partialled out by entering dummy variables for six of the seven samples used in this study. The dummy variable representing the culture omitted (to avoid singularity) from the regression run was the one showing a very low zero-order correlation with the dependent variable. This procedure allows us to show, for each adjustment and mediating variable, the resulting *beta*-coefficients associated with each substantive variables when taken in the context of the other variables and with cultural differences discounted. When the *beta* weight is multiplied by the zero-order correlation (in brackets), the amount of the adjustment variance attributable to that particular variable is ascertained. The adjustment measure's $\underline{R}^2$ represents the summed variance of all the model predictors for that outcome. As cultural differences have been partialled out, this describes the similarities across cultures of predictors of each adjustment and coping style score. We will look at cultural differences in Chapter 8.

Academic Adjustment

The first specific situation we will be modelling adjustment to is academia or school with Figure 4.1 diagramming the relationships of the demographic and mediating variables to these outcome measures.

Subjective Measures

We look first at the self-reports, starting with the child's satisfaction with school. The logic of mediated relations implies that the relation between an antecedent and an outcome is reduced when mediating variables are taken into account. An example of the effects of a mediating variable is the relationship between marks and school satisfaction. The product-moment correlation was .19, yet the *beta*-coefficient computed when all other predictors shown in the figure are considered was less than .10, and, therefore, omitted from the model. However, the *beta* weight for marks as a predictor of teacher-judged hostility, itself a predictor of child's satisfaction with school, was less affected by the other demographic predictors, the child's age and gender; with a *beta* weight of −.10 compared to a zero-order correlations of −.19. From these results one may infer that the effect of marks was largely mediated by the child's hostility, as reported by the teacher with hostility affecting satisfaction (*beta* = −.12).

In contrast, the effect of the child's age on satisfaction with school is mediated only in part by the intervening variables self-esteem, hostility and school means study. The mean correlation of age with school satisfaction is −.19 (in brackets, see Figure 4.1), and, though this drops to a *beta* = −.12 when the other variables listed above were taken into account, it still maintains a direct effect on the subjective measure of satisfaction with school. In each of our samples, older children tend to be less satisfied with school, even when the fact that older children also have lower self-reported self-esteem, lower hostility, and are less likely to feel school means study is taken into account. Though the contribution of hostility, teacher-judged, to the outcome variable satisfaction with school, seems unaffected by the presence of other mediators and demographic characteristics, there was some diminution in the effect of self-esteem in the context of other variables. The mean r of .31 between self-reported self-esteem and school satisfaction became a *beta* of .25 when child's age, teacher-judged hostility and school means study were entered into the regression equation. In contrast, though the effect of child-judged anxiety correlated −.16 with school satisfaction; its unique contribution to predicting this measure of adjustment became insignificant when in the context of other predictors.

Antecedents	Mediators	Outcomes

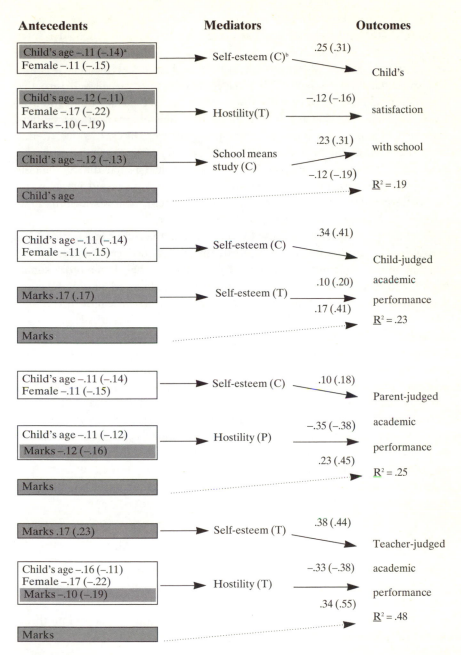

[a]   *Beta*-coefficients ≥ .10 only. Mean zero-order *r*s in brackets.
[b]   Sources: C = Child; T = Teacher.
Note: Antecedents with direct and indirect effects are shaded. Hypothesized outcomes are represented by solid lines.

FIGURE 4.1   Predictors of academic adjustment.

The mediator school means study also played a substantial role in affecting children's satisfaction with school. The more the child thought of school as having to do with study and discipline, rather than with friends and recreation, the more satisfied was the child with the institution, and this effect (mean $r = .31$) was only somewhat reduced (*beta* = .23) in the context of other variables. In turn, the main determinant of school means study was the age of the child; older children tended to emphasize studies less than friends. Though minority-group membership showed immigrants and minority respondents were likely to value studies more than friends, the *beta* was less than .10 and, therefore, excluded from the model. In the context of the other variables, gender had a small direct effect on school satisfaction (*beta* < .10), the multivariate analyses suggested a more complex pattern: girls tended to have both lower self-esteem and lower hostility than boys, which had opposite effects on school satisfaction.

From these results it makes sense to conclude that the child's satisfaction with school depended primarily on age, self-esteem, lack of hostility in the eyes of the teacher, and on imputing a predominantly scholarly, rather than interpersonal, meaning to school. These latter determinants were influenced, in turn, by male sex (enhancing self-esteem and hostility), age both directly (negatively) and indirectly, though a decline in hostility and self-esteem, and marks leading to a decline in teacher-judged hostility.

Similar logic and analysis procedures lay behind the interpretation of the other subjective aspect of academic adjustment, the child's judgment of his/her own academic performance. This outcome measure depended mainly on marks (*beta* = .17) and on the mediating variable self-esteem, as reported by the child, (*beta* = .34) and the teacher (*beta* = .10). It will be recalled that the predictors of school satisfaction were self-esteem, hostility, and the emphasis on academic rather than interpersonal aspects of school. The two outcomes differed mainly in that self-judged academic performance depended on marks as well, whereas the degree of satisfaction with school depended on the meaning of school being academic.

Objective measures

Turning to the two objective measures of academic adjustment, both parents' and teachers' judgments of children's academic performance depend mainly on the child's marks and the mediators self-esteem and (low) hostility. The small effect of the child's age was mediated by self-esteem and hostility for all three judges of academic performance, including the child's self-report shown in Figure 4.1.

The higher proportion of variance accounted for when the teacher was evaluating the performance, $R^2 = .48$ versus .25 when the evaluation was done by the parent, is undoubtedly due to the fact that all antecedents and mediators (self-esteem, hostility and, indirectly, even marks) came from the same source. The *beta* weights representing the contribution of low hostility to the positive objective measures of academic performance were similar for teachers (−.33) and parents (−.35); in both cases predictors came from the same source. In contrast, the *beta* weight of .38 for self-esteem when it came from the same source, (teachers) dropped to .04 when the child's self-report was used. The fact that no parent ratings on the child's self-esteem were available (see Chapter 3) probably accounts for the lower R^2 for parent's evaluation of academic performance. The marks' *betas* also show the same disparity, *beta* = .23 when parents judged academic performance and .17 when child-judged, in comparison to .34 for teachers. So, though the effect of source is visible in these first descriptions of predictors of objective measures of academic adjustment, the congruence between measures of identical antecedents and mediators is encouraging.

In summary, the child's academic adjustment had some different predictors, depending on the measure of adjustment utilized, but most of these effects were mediated by the personality variables, primarily self-esteem and hostility. Of the total variance accounted for, roughly two-thirds were mediated by these variables. Thus, in addition to agreeing substantially on the child's academic performance, judgments from the three sources evidently reflected two enduring personality characteristics of the child—self-esteem and hostility. In addition, and quite independently of the mediating variables, marks achieved in school were a consistent predictor of academic performance, from whatever perspective. For the dependent variable child's satisfaction with school, 89% of the variance accounted for was mediated, but here an academic meaning attributed to school was almost as important a predictor as self-esteem, while young age, rather than marks, was a direct predictor of school satisfaction.

Interpersonal Adjustment

The child's adjustment to his/her peers should depend on a somewhat different set of variables, more concerned with amiability and helpfulness than with ability. Indicators of interpersonal adjustment used here were:

1. the child's satisfaction with friends;
2. self-reported interpersonal comfort;
3. teacher-judged interpersonal competence;
4. number of recreational companions chosen from the class; and
5. number of classmates who chose the focal subject as a recreational companion.

Figure 4.2 shows the predominant predictors for all but the sociometric ratings by classmates as this outcome variable had no common predictors (significant

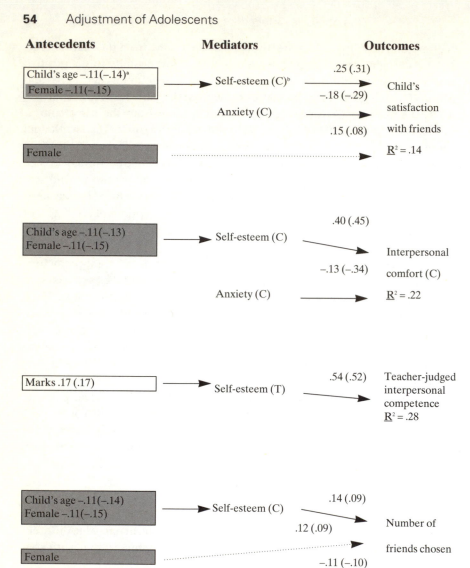

| Antecedents | Mediators | Outcomes |

FIGURE 4.2   Predictors of interpersonal adjustment.

betas ≥ .10). For all the other interpersonal adjustment measures, the personality variable of self-esteem continues to play a dominant role, though it must be noted again that the source of this predictor is consistently the same as the dependent variable. In contrast to the domain of academic adjustment, hostility is not a significant contributor to any interpersonal adjustment measures, whereas anxiety is for both self-reported satisfaction with friends (*beta* = –.18) and self-reported interpersonal comfort (*beta* = –.13). Though the self-report of anxiety was correlated with being female, having low marks, and coming from a family with lots of children, when taken together, none of their *beta* weights reached our criterion of ≥ .10. Therefore, anxiety remains, for the time being, a mediator with no significant antecedents.

Females tended to be more satisfied with their friends and choose more children from their classmates to recreate with than males (*beta* = .15 and = .12 respectively). This was in addition to the indirect effect the gender of the child had on self-reported self-esteem where females scored lower than males. So, though females were higher overall on interpersonal adjustment, this was in spite of their reporting lower self-esteem than males, itself a positive predictor of interpersonal adjustment.

Looking in more detail at the three predictors of friend satisfaction, only self-esteem is the same as those which predicted school satisfaction (Figure 4.1); friend satisfaction also depended on being female and having a low anxiety level, while school satisfaction depended on the school's being seen as a place for study and discipline, being younger and not being rated as hostile by the teacher.

The child's sense of being able to make friends and get along with others, here called interpersonal comfort, was primarily associated with self-esteem (*beta* = .40). As with satisfaction with friends, child-reported anxiety contributed negatively (*beta* = –.13) to this outcome. The only differences between predictors of interpersonal comfort and friend satisfaction were in regard to the remaining direct effect of sex. Sex had a direct effect on friend satisfaction, whereas this effect was mediated almost entirely by self-esteem for interpersonal comfort.

Teachers' judgments of interpersonal competence can be interpreted as being contaminated with their judgment of the child's self-esteem, or as being strongly determined by the latter judgment (*beta* = .54). When this self-esteem was controlled by entering other predictors and the variables representing sample difference into a multiple-regression equation, all but self-esteem had small effects (*beta* < .10), and, therefore, were deleted from the model.

Sociometric choices were not well predicted by the variables of this study. Predictors of the number of friends chosen accounted for less than 5% of the variance in this outcome measure. The expected mediating variable of self-esteem (*beta* = .14) was the only one included among the significant predictors of sociometric choice given. In addition, girls and younger children tended to choose more fellow classmates to recreate with (*betas* = .12 and –.11, respectively), than boys and older children. Though teacher-judged self-esteem was a significant predictor of the number of sociometric choices received (*beta* = .09), it was too low to meet our criterion for inclusion in a model, and, therefore, as stated above, no model for the sociometric rating received is presented here.

In summary, interpersonal adjustment, as measured by judgments from both children and teachers, depended substantially on the mediating variables, as rated by the child, of self-esteem and low anxiety. Whereas self-esteem predicted outcomes for both academic and interpersonal adjustment, for interpersonal relations low anxiety was also a predictor; for academic adjustment the additional predictor was low hostility. In addition, gender played a role in some outcomes, with female children being more interpersonally involved than males. This is a less consistent set of predictors than was found for academic adjustment, but it does show the child's self-esteem is a major determinant of adjustment.

The low variance associated with sociometric measures may have been due to the inadequacy of these measures, each depending on responses to a single question. It will also be recalled (Table 3.3) that the two sociometric indices were not highly related to other measures of interpersonal adjustment.

Family Adjustment

The domain of family relations served, in a sense, as both dependent and independent variables in this study. Family adjustment measures, used as outcomes of analysis, include the child's satisfaction with its family, the parent's satisfaction with the family, and the parent's satisfaction with the child's behaviour.

An examination of Figure 4.3 shows that the child's family satisfaction depends on all three personality variables, here used as coping behaviour mediators of adjustment. These are high self-esteem (*beta* = .27) and low anxiety (*beta* = –.14) as reported by the child, and low hostility (*beta* = –.15) as reported by the parent. The effect of age was primarily mediated by self-esteem and hostility; the direct negative effect, though significant, yielded a *beta* of only –.06 on family satisfaction and, therefore, was deleted from the model. Self-esteem decreased with age, with an accompanying *increase* in family satisfaction; whereas, though hostility also decreased with age, it was accompanied by a *decrease* in family satisfaction. The net effect of increasing age was therefore largely in the direction of decreased family satisfaction through its effect on the coping mechanisms of hostility and self-esteem. The effects of sex and school marks on family satisfaction also operated mainly through the hypothesized mediating variables of self-esteem and hostility, respectively.

The determinants of the child's satisfaction with the family were somewhat source-dependent; the child's self-esteem and anxiety were both appraised by

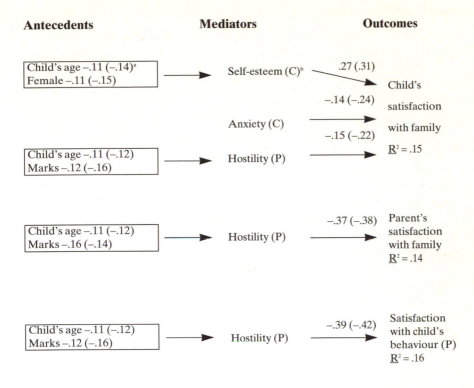

| **Antecedents** | **Mediators** | **Outcomes** |

FIGURE 4.3   Predictors of family adjustment.

[a]   *Beta*-coefficients ≥ .10 only. Mean zero-order rs in brackets.
[b]   Sources: C = Child; P = Parent.

the child, though hostility was from the parent's viewpoint. When we turn to the determinants of the parent's family satisfaction, we find it is almost completely dependent on the parent's judgment of the child's hostility (*beta* = −.37), with all the other *betas* < .10. Age and marks had an indirect effect on parental satisfaction through the effect of these demographic variables on hostility.

The parent's satisfaction with the child's behaviour depended primarily on the parent's ratings of hostility (*beta* = −.39), which mediated the effects of school marks and age. Older children and those with higher marks were rated less hostile by their parents, leading to greater satisfaction with their behaviour.

In summary, there are no direct effects of sociodemographic variables on family adjustment variables. The contribution of parent's report of (low) hostility, mediating marks and age, contributes to high family satisfaction both from the child's and parent's viewpoint. Self-esteem (child's self-report), is once again a major concomitant of child's satisfaction, and low anxiety, as with satisfaction with friends, again predicts satisfaction, this time in the family situation.

Overall Effect of Demographic and Personality Variables

Considering the determinants of the child's adjustment discussed so far, direct effects of demographic variables accounted for 4% of the variance in outcomes (that is, the product of rs and *betas* of the predictors averaged over all 12 outcome measures). In contrast, the mediating variables accounted for 16% of the variance in outcomes. The proportion of variance contributed by demographic and personality domains for each dependent variable is shown in Figure 4.4 and will be augmented as the social antecedents are introduced in the next few chapters. The most pronounced effect of demographic variables appeared for academic adjustment, where marks was the major predictor for teacher-judged academic performance. As far as mediating effects were concerned, these predominated as predictors for the rest of the adjustment measures, and, as expected, the effects of demographic variables were mediated by these personality characteristics. That is, the *beta*-coefficients associated with the remaining demographic predictors with direct effect on the outcome variables were substantially lower than their product-moment correlations. Though *beta*-coefficients for the personality predictors were, on average, lower than their corresponding rs; this decline was generally due to intercorrelations among these predictors.

Summary

The models of high-school student adjustment derived from these cross-cultural data were very similar from one sample to another, indicating that these determinants of adjustment were reasonably universal in the cultures considered. Determinants included the mediators or general coping variables considered relevant, a priori: self-esteem, anxiety, hostility, and meaning attributed to school. The higher the self-esteem, and the lower the hostility scores, the better the academic and family adjustment was likely to be if they were both from the same source. This may explain why self-esteem does not contribute to parent's ratings of the academic and family adjustment scores, as we were unable to construct a scale for parental judgment of the child's self-esteem. Contrary to expectations, hostility did not play a mediating role in predicting any of the interpersonal adjustment measures, though (low) anxiety did. Academic adjustment was facilitated by the child's view of school as being mainly concerned with study and discipline, rather than with friends and recreation. Overall, the effects of demographic variables were generally mediated by these personality characteristics, though age and marks achieved at school, had direct effects on academic adjustment, and sex directly predicted two measures of interpersonal adjustment.

The unique contributions of both the parent's and teacher's ratings of anxiety

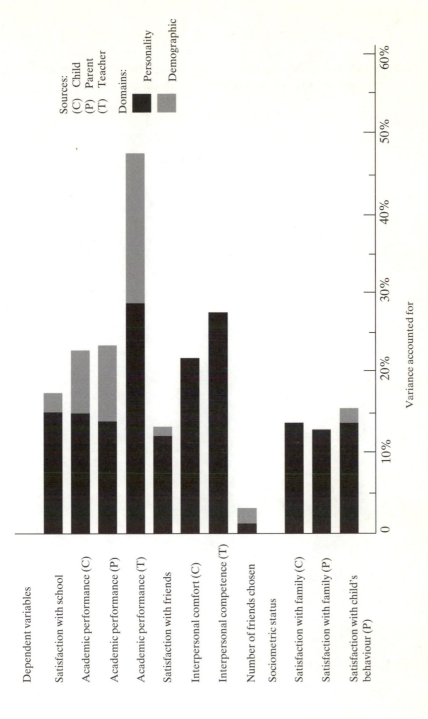

FIGURE 4.4   Percentage of variance accounted for by domain, each adjustment variable separately.

and the child's own rating of hostility were negligible (*beta* < .10) for all twelve measures of adjustment, and, therefore, do not appear in any of the models. Finally, the sex of the responding parent, the number of parent generation family members, and the family's minority-group membership did not significantly affect any of the personality or outcome variables we measured.

5

Measuring Family Relations

The child's adjustment to the family depends on his/her concurrence with parental views concerning appropriate goals and behaviour and sufficient self-control on the child's part to enact those views. It also should depend on a tolerant, supportive family style, which can accommodate occasional deviant behaviour with concern but without excessively punitive discipline. Replication of the effects of these family and child characteristics on adjustment is the subject of the next chapter. Here we are only concerned with the measurement of family practices and roles, their interrelationships and their demographic correlates.

Descriptive Measures in Present Study

Our measures of family relations were of two kinds: reported parental practices and role allocations.

Parental practices

Table 5.1 illustrates each of our measures of parental practices. The list of all items can be found in the Appendix, along with specific references to the source for each item which did not originate with us. These variables were assessed from both children and parents, with items like those used by Parker, Tupling and Brown (1979) in their Parental Bonding Instrument (PBI). Although the nurturance scales referring to mother and father could be psychometrically distinguished (their reliabilities were at least .20 higher than their intercorrelation), they had no differential correlations with other variables, so the two were collapsed. None of the other scales pertaining to the child's view of family discipline—punitiveness and protectiveness—allowed discrimination between mother's and father's behaviour.

TABLE 5.1 *Parental practices scales and sample items*

Scale[a]	k[b]	alpha[c]	Sample item
Nurturance (C)	16	.85	My father (mother) spoke to me with a warm and friendly voice.
Nurturance (P)	4	.35	I would never punish this child.
Protectiveness (C)	8	.66	My father (mother) did not want me to grow up.
Protectiveness (P)	5	.51	This child has a hard time looking after itself.
Punitiveness (C)	5	.66	My father (mother) hit me often.
Punitiveness (P)	4	.51	How often does this child get a good thrashing?

[a] Sources of measure: C = Child; P = Parent; T = Teacher.

[b] k is number of items in culture-specific scale; varied from one sample to another.

[c] Mean scale reliabilities estimates from Cronbach's alpha.

Parental nurturance

Parental nurturance was assessed from children using items from Parker's PBI (see above). Altogether there were 16 items, three direct- and five reverse-worded, with an estimated within sample scale reliability of .85. Half the items referred to the father and half to the mother, but, as noted above, they were combined for purposes of this study.

Assessment of nurturance from parents was much less satisfactory, the a priori scale containing just four items. The four items survived item analyses in only four samples, with the remaining three samples having different culture-specific scales containing just two or three items. For this reason, no common purified scale was available for analyses, and the a priori scale was used instead. There was a significant, but very small correspondence (mean within-sample r = .07) between the scales of nurturance as obtained from children and from parents. In retrospect, we infer that parental nurturance was not assessed in the parents' scale, but instead some such variable as "reluctance to punish." It does not appear as a predictor in any of the models.

Parental protectiveness

Children's items for this scale were, again, predominantly taken from Parker's PBI (scored in the direction of "over-control"). Altogether there were eight items, with an estimated mean sample scale reliability of .66.

Parents' items were intended to assess the same variable from a different perspective. The five-item scale had an estimated mean sample reliability (alpha) of .51. It correlated .22 (mean within-sample r) with the children's measure of protectiveness, from which we infer that there was some commonality in the variables assessed from the parents' and children's scales.

Parental punitiveness

Children's items for the punitiveness measure were similar in format to those in Parker's PBI, though unique to this study. The five-item common scale had an estimated reliability of .66.

The parents' common scale contained just four items, with an estimated mean sample reliability of .51. The mean within-sample correlation between parents' and children's scales was .33, from which one could infer that a similar, though by no means identical, construct was being tapped.

Role allocation

In addition to parental practices, we attempted a more objective appraisal of another aspect of family relations, namely the allocation of tasks among members. For our study we defined family relations as consisting in large part of the roles performed by members—the things each does regularly on behalf of the family, with our own a priori hypothesis that children's participation in household chores was beneficial. One could ascertain family roles by asking members such questions as, "What do you do in this group, or for this group?" (Scott and Scott, 1979). However, the lists generated from such questions vary widely from one participant to another and substantially under-report the range of roles performed.

Though it is desirable to have some standard list of common roles for respondents to peruse and indicate those which they or other members perform, one needs to apply theoretical or practical restrictions in order to keep it at manageable length. Our efforts were guided by two considerations:

1. Parsons and Bales' (1955) theory of family role differentiation, which proposes a distinction between instrumental (decision-making and economic) and expressive (socioemotional and child-related), presumably the former traditionally performed largely by males and the latter largely by females.
2. Practical knowledge of the cultures studied. Role allocations were assessed from checklists administered to both children and parents. An attempt was made to include activities common to all cultures in the sample, hence, references to lawns and cars were omitted.

The degree to which the first aim was met may be judged from the very high proportions of families in all samples in which most activities were performed by someone. The mean proportion over all 20 activities was 85%, and half of the activities elicited percentages above 90%. Lowest percentages pertained to baby-care (around 30%) and transporting of children (67%).

Although there were highly significant differences among the samples in mean performance of many roles, the mean differences over *all* activities were quite small, ranging from 78% to 90% for children, and 72% to 91% for parents. In the

Occidental samples (Berlin, Winnipeg, Phoenix and Canberra), the 20 activities were performed, on average, by 42% of the family members, while in the Oriental cultures (Hong Kong, Taipei and Osaka), an average of 25% performed them. These differential rates of participation were associated, in part, with differing family sizes, but Osaka, with a mean of 4.8 members per family, had a mean participation rate of 32%, while Canberra, with a similar mean of 4.7 members, had a mean participation rate of 43%. We will be discussing these cultural differences in a later chapter.

Each respondent was asked to make a list of family members, in order of age, and then indicate which activities on the presented list each person performed. ("Please read over the list and, if someone in your family does it, write that person's line number beside the activity. If more than one person does it, write two or more numbers beside the activity; then circle the number of the person who does it most.") From two to nine members were identified, and the mean family sizes ranged from 1.99 adults and 2.10 children in Berlin to 2.30 adults and 3.62 children in Hong Kong. Members were classified as male or female, child or adult (usually parents, but sometimes grandparents or other resident adults).

Status and maintenance roles

Several analyses of these data were undertaken. First was an empirical factor analysis to ascertain what clusters of roles existed in the sense that they were likely to be performed by the same individual. The resulting factors did not correspond clearly with Parsons and Bales (1955) typology: there was little clustering of roles by the instrumental versus socioemotional classification intended for these items, although there was certainly a strong sex differentiation in many of the roles performed.

Both children's and parents' reports of their family members' activities were subjected to principal components analyses in each sample separately. There was remarkable consistency over samples, and between children and parents, in the factors which emerged. When a particular item loaded above .50 on the same factor in all samples, it was assigned to that factor. When the dominant factor for an item differed from one sample to another, the item was excluded from the factor definition.

Composition of the factors defined by the principal components analysis for the combined sample is shown in Table 5.2. There are slight differences when the factor analyses were performed for each sample separately, because of the rather large differences in sample sizes, but the general structure is the same. The two main factors were identified as "status" and "maintenance" roles. There were nine items in the status factor, within which the most frequently performed roles were "maintaining contact with relatives" and "planning family recreation" (both intended as components of an a priori socioemotional role), but also including items concerning "discipline," "decision-making," and "community relations" (which *were* intended to represent status roles); and four items in the maintenance factor, in which the most frequently performed roles consisted of "house cleaning" and "dish washing" (which were expected to define an instrumental factor, but were restricted, instead, to certain aspects of housekeeping). Not surprisingly, the status role cluster correlated with age (mean $r = .77$), that is older members of the family were more apt to perform these roles. And, as more would expect, the maintenance role cluster correlated with sex (mean $r = .70$), with women more apt to carry out those family functions.

In addition to the status and maintenance factors, there were two items related to infant care (a rare activity in these samples). Items at the bottom of the table, which loaded on various factors in different samples, were not included in crosscultural analyses to be reported here. For instance, there was a fourth factor, designated socioemotional, which is not represented in this combined sample, though it was a factor in some samples. We shall examine in more detail these sample differences in role diffusion when we look at the effect of culture in Chapter 8.

TABLE 5.2 *Percentage of family members who performed each activity*
(2471 children, 12471 members; 1653 parents, 7725 members)

Activity	Children's Reports	Parents' Reports
Status roles		
Contact with relatives	46%	45%
Plan family recreation	38	45
Discipline the children	34	36
Make major financial decisions	34	36
Reassure family members	34	42
Plan children's education	31	37
Household repairs	30	31
Organize financial affairs	29	31
Deal with officials	27	27
Maintenance roles		
House cleaning	47	43
Wash dishes	44	49
Cooking	38	41
Go shopping for food	38	39
Infant-care roles		
Bathe the baby	9	11
Change nappies	9	11
Multiple-factor roles		
Listen to family problems	35	37
Pay bills	30	29
Take children to doctor	27	27
Take children where they need to go	24	27
Stay home with sick child	22	25

Role diffusion

The degree to which roles were distributed throughout the family may be inferred from the numbers in Table 5.2, showing the percentages of family members who were identified as performing each activity. Roles are listed within factors approximately in order of their diffusion (degree of sharing) within the families. For example, among the status (S) roles, contact with relatives was generally the most diffuse, while dealing with officials was most concentrated. Maintenance (M) roles were generally more widely shared than status roles.

Agreement between parents and children was mostly very high (except for the activities of infant-care and staying at home with a sick child), the cross-source correlation within the 20 activities of Table 5.2 averaging .84 over the seven samples. Except for "infant-care," there was considerable diffusion of roles; but the samples differed significantly in its extent, again this will be discussed in Chapter 8. Table 5.3 shows that status roles were about equally shared between the sexes, while maintenance roles were more often allocated to females than to males. Generational differences were greatest for status roles, which tended to be performed by adults about six times as often as by children. Similarly, maintenance roles were allocated to adults about twice as often as to children. There were no consistent differences in assignment of status roles to males and females. Sex differences were greatest for maintenance roles, which were more than twice as likely to be performed by females as by males. These generational and sex differences were consistently observed in all samples. As a result of these preliminary analyses we constructed a number of variables representing the frequency status and maintenance roles were fulfilled by members of the family, as reported both by the child and by the parent: Number of status and number of maintenance roles performed by the child, the adult males and the adult females. Note that the categories of adult males and females were used instead of the role performances of the responding parent to enable the contribution of both adult sexes to be covered, and, thereby, a more complete description of the functioning family.

TABLE 5.3 *Mean allocation of roles*

Report from:	To males		To females		To adults		To children	
	Parent	*Child*	*Parent*	*Child*	*Parent*	*Child*	*Parent*	*Child*
Role type[a]								
Status	3.20	3.01	3.13	2.90	5.98	5.59	0.84	0.93
Maintenance	1.08	0.88	2.30	2.29	2.36	2.18	1.19	1.18

[a] Maximum score for status roles = 9; maximum for maintenance roles = 4.

Role concentration and role differentiation

Families differed substantially from each other in the pattern of role allocation to members. Although the general trend was to assign status roles to adults and maintenance roles to females, there were many families in which role assignment was more or less restricted than this. Sometimes the mother did almost everything; in other families the mother did some things exclusively while the father did others.

The degree of sex-role concentration, that is the degree to which all roles were performed by males or by females may be represented by an index, varying between +1 (males exclusively) and –1 (females exclusively), computed as follows: female sex-role concentration = (% of roles performed by one or more males) minus (% of roles performed by one or more females).

A similar index may be constructed to represent concentration of roles in the adult generation: Adult-role concentration = (% of roles performed by adults) minus (% of roles performed by children).

To represent the degree to which males and females did different things, one may construct an index, varying between 0 and 1: Sex-role differentiation = (% of roles performed by females only) plus (% of roles performed by males only).

Similarly, the degree to which adults and children did different things may be computed as: Generational-role differentiation = (% of roles performed by adults only) plus (% of roles performed by children only). Note that roles performed by no-one in the family are not counted in any index.

Intercorrelations of Family Variables

Before examining the effect of family relations on adolescent adjustment, either directly or as mediated by methods of coping, or personality, it would seem appropriate to look at the interrelationship among these variables and their correlation with the demographic variables already entered into our models.

Table 5.4 presents the mean within-sample zero-order correlation among all the family variables, with the child's reports below the diagonal and the parent's above (see Table 2.1 for within-sample ns). In brackets on the diagonal are the correlations between child and parent for each of the 11 variables. Looking first at the relationship of family variables with source held constant, we see that nurturance is associated with low over-protectiveness and punitiveness, which go together. It is also correlated with low sex-differentiation in role allocation. Children's participation in status roles was negatively correlated with parental protectiveness, both in the child's and the parent's eyes (mean $rs = -.10$ and $-.12$, respectively). Sex-role concentration and age-role concentration were uncorrelated, but there was a tendency for sex- and age-role differentiation to go together (mean $rs = .46$ and $.43$ for child and parent); that is, families that assigned different roles to men and women tended also to assign different roles to adults and children. When sex roles were concentrated, this allocation usually obtained for adult males in status roles ($r = .67$ and $.70$) and for adult females in maintenance roles ($r = -.29$ and $-.41$). When generational-role concentration was high, it tended to be the case that parents performed both status and maintenance roles more than children.

TABLE 5.4 *Intercorrelations of family variables (mean within-sample rs)*

| | Parental practices | | | Family roles | | | | Role allocation | | | |
| | | | | Status | | Maintenance | | Age-roles | | Sex-roles | |
	Nurt.	Prot.	Pun.	Child	M Adult	Child	F Adult	Concen.	Differ.	Concen.	Differ.
Parental practices											
Nurturance	(.07*)	-.07	-.30*	.01	.03	-.03	.08*	.04	.02	.02	.05
Protectiveness	-.36*	(.22*)	.14*	-.12*	.04	-.08*	.01	.04	.08*	.01	.07
Punitiveness	-.41*	.34*	(.33*)	-.08*	.00	-.03	.00	.00	.03	-.02	.04*
Family Roles											
Child's status	.04	-.10*	-.03	(.26*)	-.29*	.30*	-.17*	-.55*	-.62*	.07*	-.25*
Male adult status	.06*	.07*	.00	-.30*	(.56*)	-.08	-.01	.33*	.30*	.70*	-.18*
Child's maintenance	.03	.01	-.02	.38*	-.13*	(.39*)	-.58*	-.50*	-.61*	.15*	-.33*
Female adult maintenance	-.03	-.02	.00	-.22*	.07*	-.59*	(.39*)	.55*	.51*	-.41*	.43*
Role Allocation											
Age concentration	.07	.01	-.03	-.51*	.36*	-.48*	.56*	(.38*)	.74*	-.07*	.20*
Age differentiation	-.07	.09*	.05*	-.58*	.29*	-.60*	.50*	.64*	(.34*)	-.14*	.43*
Sex concentration	.09*	-.01	-.01	.07*	.67*	.06*	-.29*	-.07	-.09*	(.53*)	-.50*
Sex differentiation	-.22*	.07	.09*	-.28*	-.13*	-.30*	.37*	.11*	.46*	-.41*	(.42*)

* p < .05, 2-tail. Minimum sub-sample n = 82.

Note: Children's report below numbers in brackets; parents' report above numbers in brackets; rs in brackets are child—parent correlations.

An examination of the agreement between parents and children when reporting on performance of family roles (see the numbers in brackets in Table 5.4), reveals an average correlation of .39 between parents' and children's reports of the number of status roles performed by the child and the adult female. Highest agreement (mean r = .56) pertained to male adult performance of status roles, while the lowest (mean r = .26) pertained to children's performance of status roles. Though there were differences in reports of parental practices between children and parents, discussed earlier, the overall correspondence between their family relations matrices yields a correlation of .96. The child—parent correlation similarity between the family roles and the 10 demographic variables also is very high (mean with sample r = .91). As this seems to point to a similar meaning in the family variables on the part of the children and their parents, we will only use the child's descriptions of the family when investigating the possible effect of the family roles on adjustment, though parental practices will be kept source-specific; as discussed earlier, their measures do reflect somewhat different concepts depending on the respondent.

Demographic Correlates of Family Relations

Previous research has indicated that family relations differentially affect boys and girls (Rutter, 1985) and child-rearing practices have differential consequences for the two sexes (Maccoby and Martin, 1983), with Segall (1979) attributing gender personality differences to these differential effects. Sarason, Sarason and Shearin (1986) noted that females had a negative relationship between current social support and reports of (over-) protectiveness but that there was no such finding for boys. Further, they reported this predicted family satisfaction. Slater, Stewart and Linn (1983) reported a differential effect of family disruption on adolescent males and females with the boys displaying better self-concepts and more objectivity about their family than the females. In the study of twins on which Parker's PBI was administered, Mackinnon, Henderson and Andrews (1991) reported that women twins agreed on nurturance and protectiveness whereas men did not.

The demographic correlates of our family variables are presented in Table 5.5, which shows both parent and child reports on parental practices, but only the child's for the family-role variables. Nurturance is positively associated with verbal ability and parental education for both the child and the parent reports, whereas age (both parent's and child's) is correlated only with parent's nurturance scores. Protectiveness, through both the child's and the parent's eyes, is negatively correlated with the child's age though female children report higher protectiveness scores while the parents of male children report higher scores. Punitiveness is associated with the child being young, being male, receiving low marks and displaying low verbal skills, in addition to the responding parent also being young and having little education.

TABLE 5.5 *Significant correlations between family and demographic variables (mean within-sample rs, $p < .05$)*

Demographic characteristics:	of Child				of Parent				of Family	
	Age	Female	Marks	Verbal ability	Age	Female	Education	Minority group	No. of children	No. of adults
Parental practices										
Nurturance (C)[a]	.15			.07			.16			
Nurturance (P)	-.11	.10		.13	.17		.07			
Protectiveness (C)	-.07	.10					-.10	.07	.04	
Protectiveness (P)		-.07								
Punitiveness (C)	-.13	-.11	-.12	-.11	-.10		-.06			
Punitiveness (P)	-.13		-.12	-.10	-.13		-.11			
Family roles										
Child's status role	.12					.07	.09	-.03	-.10	-.15
Child's maint. role	.12	.29		.08						-.14
Father's status role			.06		.09	-.30	.11			.34
Mother's maint. role	-.09	-.11							-.19	.10
Role allocation										
Age-role concent.	-.12		.11		-.09	-.05			-.18	.18
Age-role different.	-.18	-.14		-.09	-.06	-.08				.16
Sex-role concent.		-.13				-.28	.17		-.07	
Sex-role different.					.09		-.16			.19

[a] Sources: C = Child; P = Parent. Minimum sub-sample n = 82.

Next we turn to the correlates of status and maintenance roles, as filled by the child and male and female adults for status and maintenance, respectively. Female children are more likely to be active in maintenance roles, whereas adult males perform more status roles when the father is the respondent and when there are many adult family members. Females perform more maintenance roles when there are less children to help (mean r = $-.19$) and when the responding child is male. Participation by the responding child in both status and maintenance roles was likely to be greatest in families with few adults (mean within-sample rs with number of adults = $-.15$ and $-.14$). Maintenance roles were most likely to be performed by older female children (mean within-sample r with age = $.12$; mean r with (female) sex = $.29$).

What kinds of families are most likely to show high role concentration and role differentiation? Looking at these data in Table 5.5, we note that age-role concentration was most likely to occur when there were many adults or few children and when either the child and/or the parent respondent were young. Similar correlates were found for age-role differentiation, but, additionally, age-role differentiation is also correlated with the responding child being male and the child's verbal skills scoring low. Sex-role concentration was apt to be higher in families with many adults, when the responding adult was male, and when the parent's education was relatively high, whereas, the main correlate of sex-role differentiation was low parental education.

Summary and Discussion

Two factors included most of the 20 family roles on which data were solicited: maintenance roles (cooking, cleaning, etc., and performed primarily by women) and status roles (a composite of financial, decision-making and socioemotional tasks, and performed primarily by adults). Though children are most likely to participate in maintenance roles, their involvement in both role types depended (negatively) on the number of adults in the household, while participation in maintenance roles also depended on the child's age and (female) sex, and the child's participation in status roles depends additionally on parental protectiveness (negative relationship).

The picture we have of role concentration and differentiation in the family is of mainly structural determinants: most tasks tend to be performed by older members when there are many of them and few children or young children. Most tasks tend to be performed by one sex (usually female) when there are few adults. In addition, there are some ideological concomitants of role differentiation — namely, age-role differentiation is associated with low verbal ability of the children and sex-role differentiation is associated with low education. For the parental practices variables, we found the child's verbal ability and the parent's education level was positively correlated with nurturance and negatively correlated with punitiveness, regardless of source. If the child was female, there was a positive correlation with protectiveness and a negative one with punitiveness.

Now we are ready to look at these variables in relation to adjustment and coping behaviour as reflected in the personality variables. Again, let us emphasize that these results obtain across cultures (mean with sample $\underline{r}$s), with possible cultural differences to be discussed later.

6

Models of Adjustment: Family Relations

In Chapter 5 we examined in detail the family relations measures used in this study and their relationship to each other and the demographic variables introduced previously. The question to pursue now is whether family relations have any implications, either directly or indirectly through their effect on coping behaviour, for the child's adjustment. The particular aspects of family relations of concern here are: the parental practices of nurturance, protectiveness, punitiveness as rated by either the child or the responding parent; the child's report of the performance of status and maintenance family roles by the child, the status roles by the male adults and the maintenance roles by the female adults; and the child's description of role allocation as represented by sex- and age-role concentration and differentiation. In this chapter we will enter the family relations variables whose zero-order correlation is .10 or greater into multiple-regression analyses, along with the predictors of adjustment identified in Chapter 4. But, first, let us briefly summarize them.

Mediation by Coping Styles

Though there were many significant associations, particularly between personality and parental practices, only the child's report of nurturance and the parent's report of punitiveness had significant impact, $beta \geq .10$, when entered into regression analyses along with the previously identified demographic predictors. The $beta$ for nurturance (child's report) as an antecedent of self-esteem is .24 and for anxiety $-.27$ when the child is also the respondent. When both hostility and punitiveness are judged by the parent, the $beta$ for punitiveness is .47. Children's reports on the number of status roles performed did correlate with self-esteem and low anxiety, but none of the family role or role-allocation variables contributed uniquely to personality when the cultural effects were partialled out.

The strong support for the hypotheses that parental nurturance would be associated with self-esteem and low anxiety, and hostility with punitiveness, must be coloured by the fact that the parental nurturance measure was based on the child's judgement, as was self-esteem and anxiety, though this same nurturance variable also was a significant predictor of self-esteem as rated by the teacher. Hostility, parent-rated, does not have nurturance as a predictor, though hostility as rated by the child did. Parent's ratings of the child's hostility does have a large amount of its variance predicted by the parent's own rating of punitiveness, which has a significant negative association with parental nurturance, child-assessed. As punitiveness was the only other family relations variable besides nurturance uniquely contributing to a score of any mediator, the hypothesis that the child's coping ability as reflected by self-esteem, anxiety and hostility, is affected by parental practices received support.

Relevance for Child's Adjustment

The most pervasive result from the association of family relations to our various adjustment measures showed that parental nurturance (as judged by the child) was associated with all three kinds of adjustment — to family, to friends and to school — and from all four sources, the self-report of the child and the ratings of parent, teacher and peer (sociometric rating). Parent's punitiveness, child's judgment, also had wide ranging effects, correlating with all but sociometric status and number of friends chosen by the child. Children's self-esteem was consistently related to their own report of parental nurturance, which has been shown to affect most adjustment measures. Furthermore, the parental practices show less source effect than other predictors, that is, the magnitude of the relationship between parental nurturance, parental punitiveness and parental protectiveness and academic adjustment is similar, whether the family characteristic's report is by child or parent. An exception is the child's report on interpersonal adjustment which was correlated only with the child's report on parental nurturance. Finally, if the environmental antecedents, the coping style mediators and the adjustment outcome variables all come from the same source, the magnitude of the correlation with family satisfaction is greater when the child is the source than when all the data come from the parent.

Turning to family roles, families in which the children claimed to perform many status or maintenance activities were most likely to be interpersonally competent ($r = .10$, child-judged and $r = .08$, teacher-judged) and to choose many friends. When we look at the role allocation measures with significant correlates, age-role differentiation showed small negative relations with three measures of interpersonal adjustment (and three measures of family adjustment), suggesting that in families where parents and children performed different tasks, the children's adjustment, not only to the family, but to peers as well, was likely to be impaired. With both school and interpersonal adjustment, sex-role differentiation was negatively related (at low levels) to all measures except the sociometric status score, suggesting that families where males and females did different things were likely to have children who had difficulty interpersonally as well as academically.

When focusing on family adjustment, the types of family roles performed are related only to how satisfied the parent is with the child's behaviour. Children who perform more maintenance and status roles have more satisfied parents, while mother's high contribution to maintenance may lead her to resent the child, as represented by lower parental satisfaction with the child's behaviour. Role allocation showed a negative association to parent's satisfaction with child's behaviour for both age-role concentration and age-role differentiation; parents seem more satisfied with their children when "who does what" is not determined by generation. And, once again, we note a consistent negative correlation between sex-role differentiation and all three measures of family satisfaction.

Augmented Models of Adjustment

We start this examination of the predictive models of subjective and objective adjustment as before, with academic adjustment, followed by adjustment to interpersonal and family relations. The strategy of the analysis will be to add the family variables to the predictors already identified in Chapter 4 as having significant *betas* (Figures 4.1 to 4.3) to see if significant family *beta*-coefficients equal to or greater than .10 also emerge. In order to simplify these analyses, we will continue to base them on the composite sample (all cultures combined), but with the effects of the several cultures partialled out. In effect, this enables us to detect the effects of the predictor variables, when cultural differences are discounted. As our general model predicts the effects of family as well as demographic variables on specific measures of adjustment, to be indirect, that is, mediated by coping behaviour, the results of the regression analysis using the significant coping behaviours as outcome measures are included in these figures. Figures 6.1 and 6.2 display these relations graphically for those adjustment measures with significant augmentation from family variables. We will now examine our 12 dependent variables for possible direct and indirect effects from family characteristics as measured in this study.

Academic adjustment

Satisfaction with school

The three mediating variables, child's self-esteem, teacher-judged hostility and meaning attributed to school, continue to mediate the effects of the antecedent variables (demographic and, now, family relations), with both teacher-judged hostility and school-means-study unaffected by the introduction of family-relations variables to the regression equations. In addition, age continues to have a direct

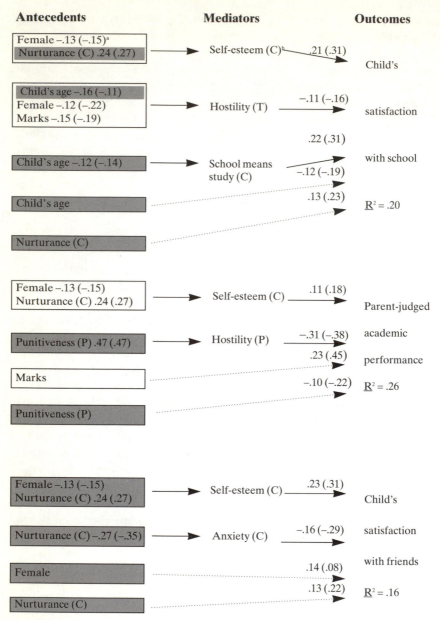

[a] *Beta*-coefficients ≥ .10 only. Mean zero-order rs in brackets.
[b] Sources: C = Child; P = Parents; T = Teacher.
Note: Antecedents with direct and indirect effects are shaded. Hypothesized outcomes are represented by solid lines.

FIGURE 6.1   Direct and indirect effects of family relations on academic and interpersonal adjustment.

negative effect on satisfaction with school. The amount of predicted variance is augmented, however, by the direct effect of the child-judged parental nurturance. Further, parental nurturance has some of its effect mediated by increasing the explained variance of the child's self-esteem. Along with nurturance, being male continues to affect self-esteem, but the *beta* for age dropped below .10 with the inclusion of nurturance and is now deleted from the model.

The direct effects, indicated by dotted lines in Figure 6.1, are contradictions to the proposed model, which states that all antecedent variables exert their influence through the mediating personality variables, as was the case for the child's sex and marks. Altogether, the three mediating variables and the two antecedent variables were associated with 20% of the variance in children's satisfaction with school; 15% was mediated through the personality characteristics specified in the model, and 5% resulted from direct effects of (presumably) antecedent conditions.

Child-judged academic performance

In contrast to the child's satisfaction with school adjustment measure, there is no direct effect of the family variables on the child's judgment of his/her academic performance, but only indirectly, through parental nurturance's effect on the self-reported self-esteem measure. The teacher's positive assessment of self-esteem is still only associated with marks , which also continues to have a direct effect on academic performance, child-judged (see Figure 4.1 in Chapter 4). Twenty-three per cent remains the variance in the outcome associated with the antecedent and mediating variables; 16% of this was mediated by the hypothesized personality variables, while 7% of effects were direct, i.e. outside the model.

Parent-judged academic performance

The predictors of parent's assessment of academic performance, including family variables, are presented in Figure 6.1. Though there was no increase in the amount of variance accounted for when family variables were included in the model for academic performance as rated by the child or the teacher, there was when it was judged by the parent. As for both the child and the teacher ratings, the effects of child-reported parental nurturance were mediated by the same source evaluation of self-esteem. Hostility, parent-judged, now mediates punitiveness, also parent-judged. Inclusion of punitiveness in the regression equation for hostility resulted in the *beta* weights for young age and low marks falling below .10 and therefore being removed from the model. Fourteen per cent of the predicted variance in parent judgments of the child's academic performance is now associated with the mediating variables self-esteem and parent's report on hostility. In addition to the child's marks continuing to have a direct effect on parent-judged academic performance, the parent's report on parental punitiveness, not only had some of its effect mediated by hostility (parent-judged), but also had a direct effect on this measure of academic performance. These two direct effects are indicated by dotted lines. The total amount of variance accounted for now raises to 26%.

Teacher-judged academic performance

Even with the introduction of family-relations variables, the principal predictors of teacher-judged academic performance remain the same: marks, both directly and mediated by both teacher-judged self-esteem and hostility, with no direct or indirect effects evident from the family variables. Figure 4.1 in Chapter 4 diagrammed these effects, showing 48% of the variance accounted for. Again, it is important to remember that the total amount of variance predicted by both mediating and antecedent variables is exaggerated by the fact that all predictors came from the teacher (self-esteem and hostility ratings plus a contribution to school marks).

Summary

Looking first at parental practices, though nurturance is significantly correlated with all four measures of school adjustment, there is a direct effect only on satisfaction with school when they are entered into regression equations along with other variables. For satisfaction with school and both child and parent-judged academic performance measures, the effect of nurturance is mediated by self-esteem. Parent-judged punitiveness has both a direct and indirect effect on parental rating of academic performance when taking into consideration the contribution of other variables. Finally, though parental protectiveness, as described by the parent, showed significant negative relations with all three measures of academic performance, none of their influence was independent of other predictors, either indirectly, as predictors of coping-style mediators, or directly onto the adjustment measures.

So we find academic performance, however judged, still depends mainly on marks and self-esteem with negative contributions from hostility, when judged by parents and teachers, with the effects of parental nurturance (child's report) mediated by self-esteem. Punitiveness has both a direct and an indirect effect (mediated by hostility) on parent-judged academic performance when both are reported by the same source, the parent. Conclusion: when family relations increased the child's self-esteem or decreased its hostility, the effect on academic performance tended to be favourable. Though the same predictors, self-esteem and low hostility, obtained for the subjective measure of satisfaction with school, in this case parental nurturance also has a direct effect. Further, with this measure of academic adjustment there is a substantial effect from the meaning the child attributes to school (academic rather than interpersonal). These findings on the positive effect from parental practices on attitudes toward and high performance in school are in line with those reported by Steinberg, Elmen and Mounts (1989).

Interpersonal adjustment

Satisfaction with friends

The mediating variables for children's satisfaction with friends remain the child's report on self-esteem and anxiety (*betas* = .23 and –.16, respectively, see Figure 6.1), with both of these coping style variables mediating parental nurturance as reported by the child. As with satisfaction with school, there is also a direct effect from the child's description of parental nurturance (*beta* = .13). It is interesting to note that, whereas none of the sociodemographic variables introduced in Chapter 4 resulted in *betas* equal or greater than .10, with the introduction of family variables, anxiety does perform its mediating function on nurturance. In addition, the direct effect of sex remains with females continuing to report higher satisfaction with friends. Altogether, 16% of the variance in friend satisfaction was associated with these predictors; 12% was mediated in ways specified by the model while 4% direct effect was noted.

Child's interpersonal comfort

In conformity with the theory that the antecedents' effect on specific adjustment measures will be mediated by personality or coping measures, the child's sense of interpersonal comfort still depends primarily on low anxiety and on high self-esteem. The family variable whose effect was mediated by these personality characteristics was parental nurturance. Though (low) parental protectiveness was hypothesized to lead to interpersonal comfort, it did not have a significant effect on it or on either of the coping variables. Altogether, 22% of the variance in interpersonal comfort continues to be associated with this set of predictors, all as implied by the model.

Teacher-judged interpersonal competence

The only mediating variable pertinent to teacher-judged interpersonal competence was self-esteem, also as judged by the teacher. This variable, a predictor confounded by being from the same source as the dependent measure, does not mediate any family variable, its only predictor remains marks. As none of the other *beta*-coefficients were substantial, all 28% of the variance is still contributed by self-esteem, teacher-judged.

Number of friends chosen

Once again, only the parental practice variable nurturance affects number of friends chosen, and all that effect is indirect, through its association with self-esteem, child-judged. No effects were large and the variance accounted for is still only 3%.

Summary

Again only nurturance has a direct effect on satisfaction, this time satisfaction with friends. It also has an indirect effect, through self-esteem and (low) anxiety, on all but the sociometric status score, and even then the zero order correlation with nurturance is significant (r = .08). Child-reported parental protectiveness and punitiveness has a negative association with satisfaction with friends and with child and teacher-judged interpersonal competence, and parent-judged punitiveness was negatively associated with low sociometric ratings. However, none of these contributed significantly to interpersonal adjustment when examined in relation to other variables.

Finally, we continue to have no predictors of sociometric status which result in *betas* ≥ .10, so there is no model for that measure of interpersonal adjustment.

Family adjustment

Child's satisfaction with family

The child's satisfaction with his/her family was most highly associated with his/her view of parental nurturance, *beta* = .59, as a direct antecedent, plus the indirect effects of nurturance as mediated by self-esteem (see Figure 6.2). Since these variables all depend on the child's report, source effects are very strong; family satisfaction must be, to some extent, synonymous with parental nurturance for these adolescents. The inclusion of parental nurturance in the regression equation lowered the *betas* to less than .10 for both the coping style measures of anxiety (child's report) and hostility (parent's report), and so these variables were deleted from the model. The total variance associated with all predictors was 43%, but only 6% was mediated by the personality variables.

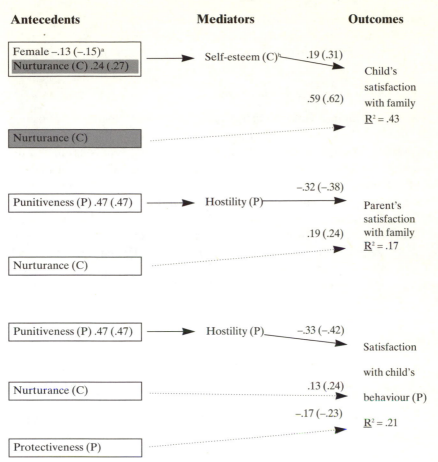

Antecedents　　　　**Mediators**　　　　**Outcomes**

Female −.13 (−.15)[a]
Nurturance (C) .24 (.27)

Self-esteem (C)[b]　　.19 (.31)

Child's
satisfaction
.59 (.62)　with family
R^2 = .43

Nurturance (C)

Punitiveness (P) .47 (.47)　　→　Hostility (P)　　−.32 (−.38)

Parent's
satisfaction
.19 (.24)　with family
R^2 = .17

Nurturance (C)

Punitiveness (P) .47 (.47)　　→　Hostility (P)　　−.33 (−.42)

Satisfaction

with child's

Nurturance (C)　　　　　.13 (.24)

behaviour (P)

−.17 (−.23)

Protectiveness (P)　　　　R^2 = .21

[a]　*Beta*-coefficients ≥ .10 only. Mean zero-order *r*s in brackets.
[b]　Sources: C = Child; P = Parent.
Note: Antecedents with direct and indirect effects are shaded. Hypothesized outcomes are represented by solid lines.

FIGURE 6.2　Direct and indirect effects of family relations on family adjustment.

Parent's satisfaction with family

The chief determinant of the parent's family dissatisfaction was the child's hostility (parent-judged), which mediated the parent's self-reported punitiveness (see Figure 6.2). Noting that there could be substantial bias in these same source reports, one may nevertheless hazard the interpretation that punitiveness produced hostile children, who diminished the parent's feeling of family satisfaction. In addition, there was a direct positive effect of parental nurturance on satisfaction, this time uncontaminated, as the predictor and outcome measures came from different sources (child and parent, respectively). Of the total 17% of variance associated with these predictors, 12% was in conformance with the model, the other 5% coming from the direct, unmediated effect of parental nurturance.

Parent's satisfaction with child's behaviour

Parental nurturance, child-rated, had a direct effect on the parent's satisfaction with the child's behaviour, along with the negative effect of over-protectiveness, as reported by the parent. As predicted, the effect of punitiveness, as rated by the parents was completely mediated by their own ratings of hostility which accounts for 14% of the variance. As we discussed earlier, the *beta* for marks, which used to be an antecedent of parents reports on the child's hostility, dropped below the cut off point of .10 and was therefore omitted. This was also true of the direct effect of marks on parent's satisfaction with the child's behaviour. When the family variables are part of the regression equation, it is also deleted from the model. Twenty-one per cent of the total variance for parental satisfaction with the child's behaviour can be predicted with the inclusion of the family variables (see Figure 6.2).

Summary

As for academic and interpersonal satisfaction, the child's satisfaction with family depends on their own report of self-esteem. Though we had hypothesized an indirect effect of parental practices, particularly nurturance, on family satisfaction, the strong direct effect shown for child's satisfaction with family and for both parent's report of satisfaction with family and satisfaction with child's behaviour, was not predicted. Note that both parental judgment of hostility and anxiety, child's report, no longer contribute enough to the variance to warrant inclusion in the model for child's family satisfaction, all replaced by the direct and indirect effect of nurturance. This is in contrast to the parent's family satisfaction measure, which still contains a major contribution from hostility, which, in turn is mediating punitiveness. It seems that parent's satisfaction with the family depends on their ratings of the child's degree of hostility, which is predicted by their own evaluation of parental punitiveness. The effect of entering family relations variables into the regression equation for the parent's satisfaction with the child's behaviour results in the parent's report on the child's hostility being augmented by direct effects from both nurturance (also child-judged!) and protectiveness, parent-judged.

Finally, contrary to expectations, there is no direct or indirect effect from any family-role performance variables on family satisfaction as reported by child or parent when these variables are entered into regression analyses along with other environmental antecedents.

Relative Effect of Family Relations Variables

As in Chapter 4, our final graph in this chapter (Figure 6.3) depicts the variance accounted for by domain of predictors. The average percentage of variance accounted for over all 12 dependent measures increased from 19% when only personality and demographic variables were included, to 22% with the inclusion of family-relation variables. Overall, the direct effect of family variables averaged 5% of the total variance; for the most part, any effect of family-relation measures was mediated by the personality variables with the exception of the three family-adjustment scales, and, to a lesser extent, the child's satisfaction with school and friends.

Summary

There were substantial source effects in most of our measures, so a summary of substantive results is most safely made from those predictors that affected all measures for a given domain of adjustment. For example, academic adjustment was assessed in four ways: satisfaction with school and the student's academic performance, as reported by the student, the parent and the teacher. When a given predictor had a significant *beta*-coefficient with three of the four outcome measures, one may be fairly certain that it was important for the student's adjustment. By this criterion, the main determinants of academic adjustment were the child's self-esteem, (lack of) hostility, and marks received. Indirectly, determinants of self-esteem and (low) hostility could be included among the determinants of academic adjustment; these were parental nurturance, being male, and, again, marks.

Altogether, there were five measures of peer adjustment, but sociometric choices was not very discriminating, so we continue with our criterion of only four outcomes significantly associated with a given predictor. This yields self-esteem, with a direct effect and parental nurturance (indirect except for satisfaction with friends) and being female as fairly consistent determinants.

Family adjustment was measured by three outcomes. The two which depended on parent rating were significantly affected directly by the child's hostility (in the parent's eyes), parental nurturance (in the child's eyes), and, indirectly, through its effect on parent-judged hostility, punitiveness (as reported by the parent). Parental nurturance, as judged by the child, had a direct effect on all three measures, with self-esteem also contributing to the increase in variance predicted for the child's satisfaction with the family.

Self-esteem was clearly the most consistent predictor of adjustment to all of these three foci of adjustment. Hostility was a (negative) predictor of adjustment to school and to family. Marks were a distinctive predictor of school adjustment, while parental nurturance was a distinctive predictor of family adjustment, with

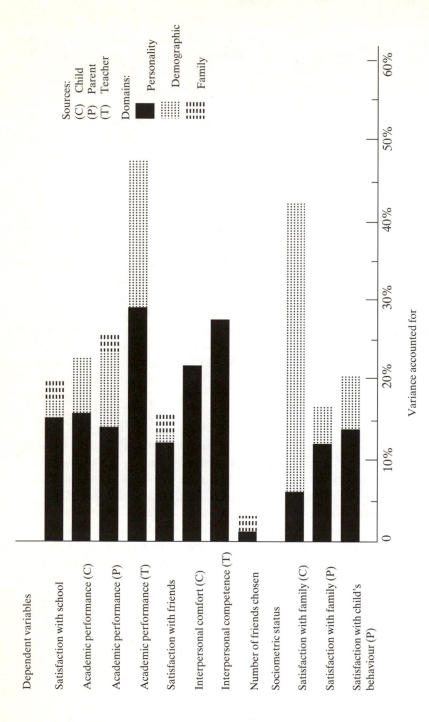

FIGURE 6.3   Percentage of variance accounted for by domain, each adjustment variable separately.

effects both direct and mediated by self-esteem. In all four cases, one should note that the direction of effects is ambiguous. High self-esteem may result from, or lead to, good adjustment. Hostility may be a reaction to, as well as a cause of, academic and family adjustment. High marks may result from, as well as induce, good academic adjustment. And parental nurturance may result from, as well as produce, acceptable home behaviour in the child. Despite the fact that one cannot infer causation from cross-sectional data, we think it would be fruitless to attempt any kind of experimental, or even longitudinal, approach to the question of direction, for it must certainly be bi-directional, with these measures of outcome having recursive effects on their mediating, and even antecedent, conditions.

Finally, it must be noted that the role allocation and dispersion within the family had insignificant bearing on any of our measures of adjustment, when we looked for predictors that obtain in all seven samples or cultures. Yet, sex-role differentiation was negatively related (at low levels) to measures pertaining to all three sorts of adjustment, suggesting that families where males and females did different things were likely to have children who were maladjusted to one focus or another. When we get to the discussion of possible effects on adjustment using cultural norms, we will be bringing these variables back into the picture again. Certainly, the preponderance of increased variance attributed to family relations in the domain of family adjustment in contrast to school or interpersonal adjustment, is rational.

7

Models of Adjustment: Similarity to Peers

To date, we have looked at the demographic antecedents of adolescent adjustment either directly or indirectly, through their effect on coping styles. We have then moved on to describe the impact of the family environment on the various facets of adjustment viewed either through self-report or as judged by others. An additional source of environmental influence for our students is that generated within the classroom. So the next influence on adaptation we wish to address comes from the classmates with whom they interacted. Though the issue of relative influence from peers and parents is of theoretical interest, comparison of parent—child similarity with peer—child similarity is only possible in our study for the ranked importance of areas of concern: recreation, community, possessions and environment (one question), so have been ignored.

In any class one would accept that students would select only some members with whom they wish to associate. For our purposes, we defined each student's friends as those she/he nominated or were nominated by as someone to recreate with (see description of sociometric status in Chapter 3). As we limited the choice of friends to those in the class, we use the word "peer" to represent the classroom influence on adjustment. As we discussed in Chapter 1, increased similarity between a respondent and his/her friends is associated with the strength of the traits, so one would expect the traits most important would be those on which his/her friends were also high. Therefore, measures representing the peer—respondent similarity on the variables included in this study were calculated. However, there is evidence in the literature that some traits reflect objective criteria of status, for instance marks and sociometric status, which attract those who are lower on that characteristic, so we have also included the mean score of the peers on these objective variables to represent this alternative reason for selection of friends. As an example of these two scores reflecting possible peer influence, if a child had low marks and his/her nominated peers' marks were high, the mean peer mark score would be high, and the peer—child mark similarity score would be low.

In addition to calculating mean peer scores and respondent mean peer similarity scores for the dependent, antecedent and mediating variables already covered in previous chapters, items measuring the importance of school, friends, job, recreation, community, possessions and the environment from both the child and parent were included to represent the domain of interests and attitudes. The Appendix has a detailed listing of the items making up these variables.

Predictors of Similarity

Overall, all but two of the 68 mean correlations between respondent and mean peer are positive, indicating that a respondent chooses and is chosen by peers who are very like him/her. Furthermore, 65% show significant zero-order mean within-sample correlations between the focal subject's score and the mean score of peers. Similarity scores are grouped by domain: the personality traits or coping styles, demographic variables, family relations, attitudes or interest orientations and, finally, the dependent measures of adjustment. The similarity variables can be further distinguished by the source of information: the child, the parent or the teacher. Figure 7.1 summarizes graphically the relationship between the respondent-mean peer similarity score and the magnitude of the respondent's response on that variable, grouped by domain and source. The greatest similarities were on demographic characteristics and teacher-judged personality, and, to a lesser extent, adjustment. Further down the list of similarities were children's attitudes, family relations, and parent-reported characteristics of the children and their families.

With a significant F ratio of 4.95, the mean similarity correlates were tested for significant ($p < .05$) domain differences using Newman-Keuls. Though the mean similarity correlate of .30 for all demographic variables, regardless of source, is significantly greater than those of all the other domains, none of the other mean similarity scores can be distinguished within the 5% probability of significance, even when controlling on source. Highest among the demographic entries were age and sex, even when same-sex classes were removed from analysis. In choosing friends, the importance of demographic characteristics, particularly the emphasis on same-sex friends, was also pointed out by Kandel, Davies and Baydar (1990) in their analyses of adolescent dyads. Other high similarity variables were average marks received on subjects at this school and verbal ability as measured by the Cloze Test (Taft and Bodi, 1980). This similarity was contributed in part by some schools' practice of streaming students into ability levels, making choice of same-ability friends more likely. A major limitation of the population from which friends could be nominated meant that we could not ascertain the potency of proximity in friend selection.

If one looks at all domains of variables combined, by source of information, there is a low level of similarity on variables from parents of the respondent in relation to parents of the child's peers (mean within-sample $\underline{r}$ = .09) as compared to the respondent's and mean peer teacher (mean $\underline{r}$ = .26) and child (mean within-sample $\underline{r}$ = .18). With a significant $\underline{F}$ ratio of 3.84 ($\underline{p}$<.05), The Newman-Keuls analysis designated the parent mean significantly lower than both the teacher and the child mean $\underline{r}$, $\underline{p}$<.05, but denoted no significant difference between child and teacher data source. Children are, of course, more able to sample characteristics of their friends as they see them often and it is the same for the teachers who are rating both the child and his/her peers, so it is not a surprising finding. In fact, one would be surprised if it were not so. Kandel, Davies and Baydar (1990) also found lower agreement for their salient dyads on parent relations than for school-related activities.

Thus, our data seem to support the conclusion of previous research (see Chapter 1) that children's choices of friends are based more on similarity in gross demographic characteristics, such as sex, and obvious manifestations of personality characteristics that the teacher can judge than on similarity of attitudes and family relations. Teacher-judged characteristics of the child—hostility, anxiety, self-confidence, and academic performance—were more likely than self-reported or parent-judged characteristics to show similarities within friendship groups. This may be because of teachers' tendencies to see similarities among students who go together, an example of Heider's (1958) well-known phenomena of cognitive balance, or it may reflect their use of a common—hence more accurate—frame of reference (e.g. all the children she/he has taught) when judging a large number of children.

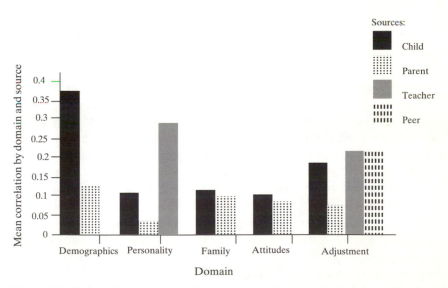

FIGURE 7.1 Respondent's score magnitude and peer-similarity correlations by domain and source.

Correlates of Similarity with Peers

Though there was no overall relationship between the magnitude of the characteristics being measured and the tendency either to select or to avoid children similar to themselves ($r = -.06$), there were substantial differences among the variables under consideration. From this we can conclude that there were specific variables where child—peer similarities and dissimilarities seem to be an important source of selection or influence. For instance, minority-group members were likely to be in majority-group friendship circles, rather than in ethnically solitary units, represented by a negative r between the similarity score and the strength of the child's score. Children with high verbal skills were more likely to select friends who were also verbally skilled than were children with low skills.

Just as Back (1951) found that friendship choices tend upward in the status hierarchy of experimental groups, so we found that children tended to select as friends classmates who came from families with superior parental practices. This is shown in a tendency toward similarity between friends in desirable family characteristics, but dissimilarity in undesirable characteristics. For instance, children with nurturant parents and satisfying family relations tended to choose friends whose parents were similar in these respects; but children whose parents were restrictive (over-protective) or punitive tended to choose friends whose parents were otherwise. The correlation between strength of nurturance and family satisfaction scores and similarity to mean peer score was .28 for the former and .44 for the later. In contrast, the strength of parental protectiveness and similarity to mean peers on that variable was $-.19$, and for parental punitiveness, $-.34$. The source for all of these data was the child, significant at $p < .01$, 2-tail. Later in the chapter we will see if these peer-similarity scores, are, in fact, associated with increased adjustment, when considered along with the demographic and family variables already introduced into the models.

Turning to the family role characteristics, generational role differentiation in the family led to a choice of friends in similar circumstances, but sex-role differentiation did not show similar selective effects. Children who come from households where the father is the one who usually fills the status role pick friends who come from similar households. However, roles which cannot be shared, as is the case for nominees for the one who fills the status roles or sociometric ratings of popularity, are instances in which similarity does not obtain when picking friends, rather, the reverse holds, one picks those unlike one. This means that children who perform status roles pick friends who do not, and children low on sociometric ratings pick friends who were high. Importantly, all these results hold regardless of whether the comparison is between the child and the mean peer child response or the parent and the mean parent response.

In the area of personality, this impetus to select like friends on desirable characteristics if one is high on the trait oneself, i.e. self-esteem, but unlike ones for those less desirable traits, i.e. anxiety and hostility, holds regardless of source of information, and, overall, family and adjustment variables are much more likely to be associated with similarity scores than are attitude or interest characteristics. Demographic and personality variables are indistinguishable (non-significant, using Newman-Keuls to determine significant group differences) from other domains on proportion of similarities associated with them.

Adjustment and Peer Similarity

Adjustment of students was generally affected by their similarity to friends. Data on these relationships appears in Figure 7.2. Well-adjusted children were more likely than the poorly-adjusted to select friends at the same level as themselves on a particular outcome measure. Out of 12 comparisons this difference was significant in 8, with no instances in the opposite direction. The parents not only do not show high similarity between respondent and peer, as shown in Figure 7.1, their description of their child's adjustment is less influenced by any respondent—peer similarity scores than either the children's or the teachers' rating of adjustment. Figure 7.2 depicts the proportion of respondent-mean peer similarities *within* each domain, which were significantly correlated with each of the dependent variables.

Considering each adjustment measure separately, friends who were high on these tended (at $p < .05$) to be like one another, more than non-friends, on all outcome measures; a similarity in 15% of the predictors for academic and family adjustment measures compared to 22% for interpersonal measures. When we look at respondent—peer adjustment similarity only, the proportion of significant similarity scores for the three areas of adjustment is 21% for academic measures, 28% for family and 33% for interpersonal measures. The bases of similarity most closely related to adjustment were number of friends nominated, satisfaction with family and sociometric popularity.

One reasonable interpretation of these results is that adjustment of students is enhanced by having friends who are themselves at a high level of adjustment. Another interpretation is that well-adjusted students are best able to select friends whose characteristics they share. These are likely to be demographic characteristics, such as sex and verbal ability; and academic performance as well as other levels of adjustment and personality characteristics displayed in the classroom, such as self-confidence, hostility and anxiety. Our preference for the latter interpretation stems from the fact that the degree of similarity in correlates varies over the several measures of adjustment, with sociometric and other interpersonal measures being among the highest, with the primary direction toward increased adjustment being associated with similarity in peer scores, especially in the interpersonal arena.

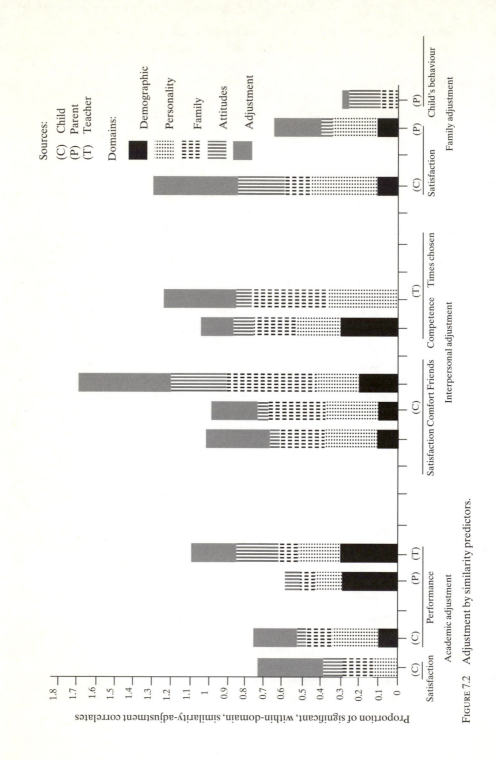

FIGURE 7.2 Adjustment by similarity predictors.

The Contribution of Peers to Predicting Adjustment

To systematically test whether additional information about peer similarity could contribute to the amount of variance accounted for on the 12 adjustment measures used in our study, we followed the same procedures outlined in the previous chapter when we added the family values to our model. Here we used the similarity measures whose mean within-sample scores were significant. Though Ide, Parkerson, Haertel and Walberg (1981) propose the child peer similarity scores as the main influence, we felt that there was evidence from our own data, that selecting peers with higher mean scores than their own (also see Berndt, 1989) can also be a significant factor. Therefore, we entered those mean peer variables, again, if their correlation with the dependent variable was significant at the .05 level. Finally, we also entered the 14 new attitudinal and interest variables as represented by the importance of various areas of interest to the parents or children, if, again, the mean within-sample scores were significantly related to the dependent variable in question.

As in the previous models of antecedents of adjustment presented in Chapters 4 and 6, the possible increments due to peer and attitude variables to the explained variance for our dependent measures (the *betas*), is with the idiosyncratic culture or sample contribution also entered into the equation, but excluded from the reported R^2 or predicted variance.

The mediators

Before proceeding to looking at the effect of the peer and attitude variables on our outcome measures, we will first look at their relationship to our mediators, the coping styles. Of the six mediators still affecting adjustment, two, child-judged anxiety and parent-judged hostility, were not influenced by respondent — peer similarity, mean peer, or attitude/interest scores when they were added into the regression equation along with the previously determined antecedents from the demographic and family domains. However, adding the peer similarity score on subjectively reported self-esteem to the predictors of the child's self-esteem (*beta* = .10), increased its known variance; it now is included, along with being male and coming from a family with high nurturant parental practices. The self-esteem, teacher-judged, variance increased 11% by knowing the peer similarity of the teacher-judged self-esteem and anxiety. These similarity scores do not effect the contribution of marks to this score. Obviously, the teacher judges the child's friends to exhibit similar personality traits.

Turning to another mediator of the antecedents of adjustment, the indirect effect of mean peer hostility scores given by the teachers affects the teacher's hostility scores on the child. This, along with a positive contribution from the child's report that friends are important, adds marginally to predicting the teacher's rating of hostility along with being male, which continues to be a predictor. On the other hand, the inclusion of these new variables resulted in the *betas* for both marks and age dropping below .10; these two demographic variables were, therefore, dropped from the models involving teacher-rated hostility. We interpret these findings to mean that teachers will judge a child to be hostile if they run around with other children they view as hostile and if the children value friends as very important, in addition to the already known predictor of being male.

Finally, school means study (child's report) now mediates a *low* rating to the importance of friends and a high rating of the importance of school in place of (young) age, as in the models in Chapters 4 and 6. Young adolescents are more apt to view school as meaning study, but also think schooling important and friends less so. Note that the measure of importance of friends is independent (no overlapping items) of the mediator school means study not friends, though the mean within sample r was –.36.

Now, we are ready to look at the effect of peers on our children's adjustment. Taking each of the 12 dependent variables in turn, we start with the domain of academic adjustment.

Academic adjustment

Figure 7.3 shows the modest increase, 3% when compared to Figure 6.1, in variance accounted for in the child's satisfaction with school when their similarity to nominated peers on this subjective adjustment variable is known. Being young and from a nurturant family also continue to have a direct effect. Self-esteem, child-judged, makes a major contribution to predicting this adjustment measure, mediating the child's sex and, partly mediating parental nurturance, which also continues to have a direct effect. This supports the finding of Gavin and Furman (1989) who found there was a greater similarity between younger adolescents and their peers than with older ones. Lackovic-Grgin and Dekovic (1990) found this particularly in regard to self-esteem. Our data seem to bear this out; the effect of younger children having lower self-esteem, self-report, is mediated by the fact that younger children associate with those who have similar self-esteem.

All told, we can account for 23% of the variance for the child's satisfaction with school; with only 7% being direct antecedents, and the remaining 16% mediated by the three variables self-esteem, low hostility and school means study.

Moving on to the other measure of school adjustment, academic performance, there was no direct effect on the child's, parent's or teacher's own evaluation of the child's academic performance by peer-similarity or attitude scores; only indirectly, through the effect on self-esteem (child or teacher), or hostility (teacher-judged only). Hostility, as rated by the parent remains a predictor of parent's judgment on the child's academic performance, and does not mediate any of the peer related variables.

Antecedents	Mediators	Outcomes

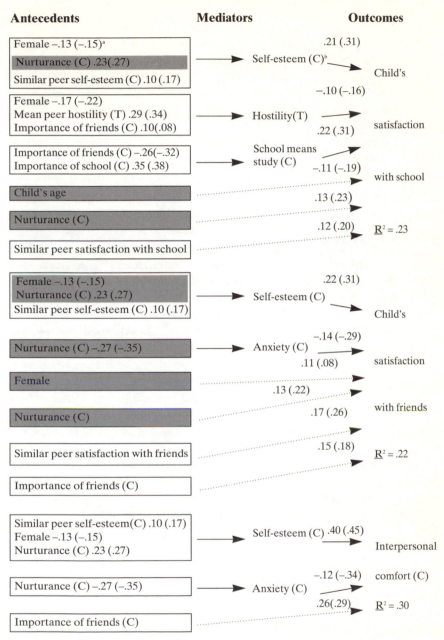

FIGURE 7.3   Direct and indirect effects of peers on subjective measures of academic and interpersonal Adjustment.

Summary

For all three academic performance measures, all the peer and interest variables tested for inclusion in the models relating to academic adjustment were mediated by self-esteem and hostility. Only for the child's satisfaction with school does a similarity with peer variable (satisfaction with school itself), contribute to the amount of variance explained in all seven cultures. However, the importance adolescents place on various facets of their lives also affected academic adjustment. Not only did the importance of friends effect the child's satisfaction with school indirectly through its negative correlation with school means study, its effect was also mediated by teacher-judged hostility when the teacher evaluated academic performance.

Interpersonal adjustment

As mentioned earlier, all five measures of interpersonal adjustment are affected by knowledge about peer characteristics in relation to the respondent and also by information about the respondent's own areas of interest and concern. We see the predictive variance of child's satisfaction with friends increasing from 16% to 22% with 11% mediated and 11% directly predicted by the antecedents (see Figure 7.3 in comparison to Figure 6.1 in Chapter 6) with the introduction of the child's own report of the importance of friends along with the child—peer similarity in their satisfaction with friends.

Though family variables did not increase the predicability of any objective interpersonal adjustment measures, the child's report of interpersonal comfort, shown in Figure 7.3, shows that the attitude variable importance of friends contributes directly to this adjustment score. The introduction of this variable accounts for the 8% increase in variance to 30%, in comparison to the model in Figure 4.2 where the R^2 of 22% was solely the result of the mediating variables self-esteem and anxiety, both child-judged.

Moving on to objective measures of interpersonal adjustment, the model in Figure 7.4 shows 35% of the teacher-judged interpersonal competence score accounted for, an increase of 7% from the model in Figure 4.2, when its only predictor was teacher-judged self-esteem. The increment resulted from the addition of information about the similarity of the child with his/her peers on interpersonal competence, teacher-judged.

The number of friends chosen by the child shows peer influence with the variance accounted for rising to 10% from a mere 3% (Figure 7.4). In addition to placing great importance on friendship, being able to pick peers with high sociometric standing also contributes to the number of friends chosen. These peer-related variables replace the demographic variables age and sex previously appearing in the model in Figure 4.2. We have already observed the negative relationship between importance of friends and age. Note that being female does not predict sociometric status per se, so the effect is more likely that females select their friends on the basis of popularity more than males. As the variance accounted for by including the peer-related variables is substantially greater than when sex and age were the only direct predictors, one must conclude that peer relations represents more than its demographic predictors. Only 1%, out of the 10% predicted, was mediated by self-esteem, with the remaining 9% attributed directly to mean sociometric status and importance of friends.

Finally, the first significant predictor of the interpersonal adjustment variable, the sociometric rating, emerges but only with the inclusion of mean sociometric of the peers doing the nominating (Figure 7.4), and even then we end up predicting only 6% of the variance. We would assume, from previous research, that those with high sociometric status—a higher number of choices by others—

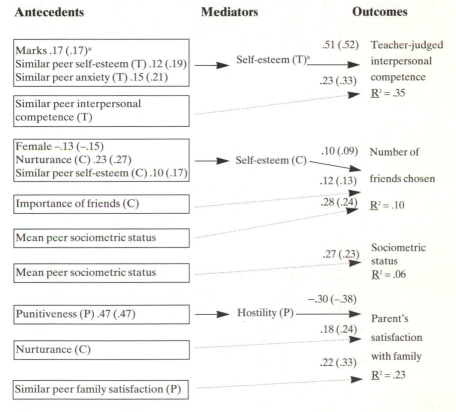

Antecedents   **Mediators**   **Outcomes**

Marks .17 (.17)[a]
Similar peer self-esteem (T) .12 (.19)   Self-esteem (T)[b]   .51 (.52)   Teacher-judged
Similar peer anxiety (T) .15 (.21)   interpersonal
                                                          .23 (.33)   competence
Similar peer interpersonal $R^2 = .35$
competence (T)

Female −.13 (−.15)
Nurturance (C) .23 (.27)   Self-esteem (C)   .10 (.09)   Number of
Similar peer self-esteem (C) .10 (.17)   friends chosen
                                                          .12 (.13)
Importance of friends (C)   .28 (.24) $R^2 = .10$

Mean peer sociometric status
                                                          .27 (.23)   Sociometric
Mean peer sociometric status   status
                                                                           $R^2 = .06$

                                                          −.30 (−.38)
Punitiveness (P) .47 (.47)   Hostility (P)   Parent's
                                                          .18 (.24)
Nurturance (C)   satisfaction
                                                          .22 (.33)   with family
Similar peer family satisfaction (P) $R^2 = .23$

[a] *Beta*-coefficients ≥ .10 only. Mean zero-order rs in brackets.
[b] Sources: C = Child; P = Parent; T = Teacher.

FIGURE 7.4   Direct and indirect effects of peers on objective measures of interpersonal and family adjustment.

would be negatively correlated to the status of those doing the nominating (Back, 1951). However, it seems from our data that when the sociometric choice, based on popularity for recreational partners, was made, those who were most popular belonged to peer groups of equally popular members, and those who were not, chose others to recreate with who were equally unpopular.

Summary

Once again, as with satisfaction with school, the child's satisfaction with friends is in part determined by the similarity of satisfaction with friends of her/his selected peers. In addition, the importance the child places on friendship has a direct effect not only on satisfaction but also on the more objective measures of self-reported interpersonal comfort and number of friends chosen, and the teacher's rating of interpersonal competence is influenced by the competence of her/his friends. Last, the sociometric status of their peers predicts not only how many they choose, but also how many nominations they get as possible recreational partners.

Family adjustment

Interestingly, the child's satisfaction with family shows no direct effect from peers; only the indirect effect of associating with peers with similar self-reported self-esteem which is entirely mediated by self-esteem (see Figure 6.2 in Chapter 6 for the last representation of the model of child's satisfaction with family).

Turning to the objective family adjustment variable represented by parental satisfaction with family, Figure 7.4 shows an increase from 17% to 23% in the total amount of variance accounted for by the inclusion of the measure representing the similarity between the parents of the peers and the parent of the adolescent under study on satisfaction with family. The proportion of the variance accounted for by this similarity variable alone is a bit less than half of that contributed by the mediator parent-judged hostility.

Lastly, the predicted variance of satisfaction with child's behaviour remains at 21%, unaffected by peer or interest variables, with two-thirds of the variance mediated by hostility, parent-rated, and the other third by direct antecedents: the family variables (low) protectiveness and (high) nurturance.

Summary

For the child's satisfaction with family, the peer effect was indirect, as predicted; the higher the mean peers' similarity to the child's self-report on self-esteem, the higher the child's self-esteem score. Parent's family satisfaction was higher if the child had friends whose parents also were satisfied, but is influenced primarily by parental reports of child's hostility, (low) parental over-protectiveness, and the child's reports of a nurturant family.

Relative Effect of Peer Variables

Figure 7.5 shows the relative, overall contribution to the explained variance from the demographic, personality, family and, now, the significant peer and attitudinal variables introduced here. One is immediately struck with the continued importance of the antecedent and mediating effects of demographic and personality variables in predicting adjustment, even with the inclusion of social environmental variables relating to family and peers when predicting academic adjustment. Again, not surprisingly, family variables continue to contribute substantially, but only to those adjustment variables having to do with the children in relation to the family, and, to a lesser extent, the school. The exception is with satisfaction with family, from the parent's standpoint, where a significant predictor of this is the parents of their children's friends having a similar degree of satisfaction with their families. With the introduction of the peer and attitudinal variables, it is in the area of interpersonal adjustment where increases, though modest, are most evident.

Summary

There were distinctive patterns of inter-friend similarity. Children who chose one another were more likely to be of the same sex, verbal ability, and academic performance levels than non-friends, and more likely to be judged similar in personality characteristics (self-esteem and hostility) by their teachers. Self-reports of these same three personality characteristics, however, were scarcely more similar than chance within friendship pairs. Friends tended to be similarly satisfied with school and similarly concerned with interpersonal relations. However, there was no general tendency to choose friends on the basis of similarity in all respects; notably, family relations were not especially similar between pairs of friends. Rather, there was a tendency for most children to choose friends whose families displayed desirable interpersonal characteristics, such as nurturance and parental satisfaction. Unhappy children in unfortunate family circumstances did not tend to choose each other. The best adjusted children tended to have friends with the most desirable characteristics, similar to themselves, such as many friends, satisfaction with their families, and other aspects of adjustment. Conversely children high on undesirable traits or low on status-ranked roles, including sociometric rank, picked peers unlike themselves.

We could not test the potency of proximity as a selection criteria (see Epstein,

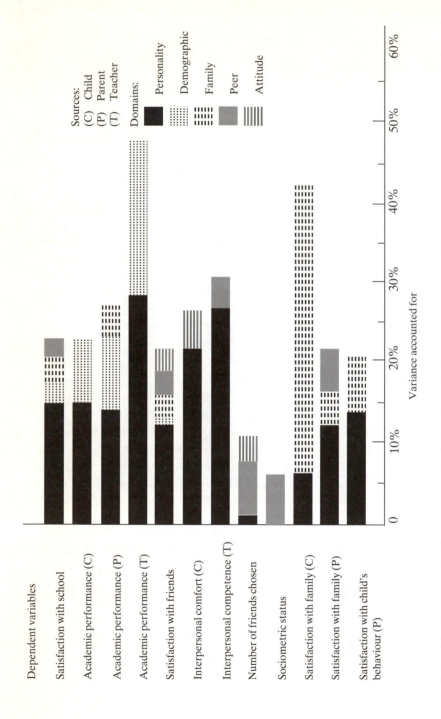

FIGURE 7.5 Percentage of variance accounted for by domain, each adjustment variable separately

1989; Festinger, Schachter and Back, 1963) as choices were limited to those from the same class, but the dominance of demographic or background variables and personality characteristics in peer-similarity characteristics rather than attitudes or interests supports Epstein's (1989) description of the developmental bases for friendships, whereby friends are secondarily culled from proximity selected acquaintances using this more accessible information. Finally, adjustment in the interpersonal area is more influenced by peers than academic or family adjustment, much of the effect mediated by personality. Overall, the knowledge about interests or attitudes, particularly the importance of friends (child's report), and about the stance of peers on various variables, does contribute some predictive power to levels of adjustment, especially in the area of interpersonal adjustment, but nothing in comparison to the amount contributed by demographic and personality variables. However, it does seem that, irrespective of the adjustment domain, a similar level of satisfaction is a criterion for selection of friends, and overall importance of having friends is a concomitant of competence in interpersonal relations. For the relatively more objective measures, peer effect is only indirect for academic performance. We shall now proceed to our final predictors, namely the role of the culture in which subjects are embedded.

8

Models of Adjustment: Cultural Impact

What is one to make of sample differences? An error term is usually defined as a non-concordance between a hypothetical construct and the operational definition of variable. Do we attribute our error terms to translations which resulted in different meanings of the variables in different samples, different kinds of respondents selected from the several cultures, or actual differences in average response levels representing cultural differences in demographic, family or peer characteristics? We propose to examine error in terms of its cultural specific aspects to see if we can reduce unaccounted variance or error term for our measures of adjustment.

Effects of Culture on Dependent Variables

Poortinga and Malpass (1986) use the term "culture" as another social environment variable, so, as a final contribution to our models of predicting adjustment, we will look at the effects the cultural norm has on individually measured variables. Thus the significance of the respondent's position on the predictor in comparison to those in the culture as a whole, is assessed. Rutter, Yule, Quinton, Rowlands, Yule and Berger (1975) used independently obtained socioenvironmental variables in their study of attainment and adjustment in two geographical areas. Independent measures were unavailable in this study, so we used the sample or cultural mean of predictor variables to test whether or not the cultural level, in addition to the individuals response, would increase the amount of variance accounted for. Remember that by culture we mean the immediate environment of the child as our samples were not random samples of the cities in which the data were collected.

We will now review the models of each of our outcome variables in light of the cultural specific differences that are associated with each sample. In keeping with the general procedure followed in the analyses presented in this book, only cultural variables with *betas* $\geq$ .10 will be entered into these final models of variables associated with our 12 measures of adjustment. It is important to keep in mind that the *beta* weights representing the coping style mediators and the antecedents classified under the sociodemographic, family and peer domains are unaffected by these cultural means as they are substituting for the sample dichotomies used to control for the variance attributed to only sample differences. There will be instances where we were unable to specify the variables affecting judgment and, therefore, have to represent the cultural effect with a dichotomous variable with a *beta* $\geq$ .10. We will leave a description of the specific similarities and differences in our samples until after an examination of the cultural effects on our models of adjustment.

Before looking at adjustment, we will first summarize the cultural effects on our mediating variables, the coping styles of self-esteem, anxiety and hostility, and the orientation variable, school means study.

The mediators

Looking first at school means study, the amount of predictive power added by the cultural variables raised the amount of variance accounted for from 22% to 30% with the addition of the cultural norms on the child's ranking of importance of friends, parental (over-) protectiveness (parent's report), and family sex-role differentiation scores. These predictors were in addition to the contribution of the measures of importance of friends and school which were common to all cultures. In our sample, cultures where children are less likely to value friends, come from homes where parents are more likely to be over-protective, and come from homes with low division of roles based on sex, are more likely to view school as meaning study than as a place to make friends. In this regression analysis, the dichotomous representations of unspecified sample differences continued to be present, however none of the *betas* were .10 or higher so, as is our practice, are not reported and left as representing unaccounted-for variance.

Next we examine the coping style self-esteem, first based on the child's self-report. To the 10% variance previously accounted for, the cultural norms add a further 15% with the inclusion of the positive effect of the cultural norms on importance of friends and the negative effect from the family age-role differentiation (*betas* of .27 and −.24, respectively). These two cultural effects on self-esteem augment the effect of being male, having nurturant parents and associating with others who report similar self-esteem levels. The impact from the cultural norms on the child's self-esteem as evaluated by the teacher also has imput in addition to the stable effect over all samples from marks and similar peer self-esteem and anxiety, pinpointed by within-culture analyses. Teachers from cultures with high parental education and a higher proportion of families from minorities rated self-esteem higher. The teachers also were more likely to rate the child's self-esteem higher if the culture norm for similar interpersonal competence (teacher-judged) among peer groups was also higher.

Turning to the mediator anxiety, based on self-report, in addition to the contribution of parental nurturance to low anxiety in all samples, knowing that the child is in a culture with high overall parental nurturance contributes 7% to the amount of variance explained for the measure of anxiety. Even after specifying some of the between-sample variance to parental nurturance, we are still left with a *beta* of –.12 attributable to something unspecified about the Canberra sample, which led to lower anxiety scores for those children. This contributed significantly (2%) to the overall variance.

Finally, we examine the effect of cultural norms on our measures of hostility. Interestingly, there is no culturally-specific effect when the child's hostility is based on the parent's judgement; all the measured variance accounted for is based on one variable, parental punitiveness, which was found in all seven samples. When hostility is based on the teacher's judgment, however, there is a contribution from cultural differences. When the child comes from a culture with low parental education, the teacher is more likely to rate the child as hostile. This was the only addition to the predictors found in all samples: being male, having high-mean hostility ratings from the teacher to the peers of the child, and having the child rate the importance of friends high. The increase in variance accounted for by including the culture's mean on parental education was 3%. We will discuss the implications of these findings in the context of the various adjustment measures in which they act as mediators of sociodemographic, family, peer and cultural variables.

Academic adjustment

Satisfaction with school

In the previous chapters, we have only been interested in comparable results across all seven samples. Having established the common antecedents of adjustment, we are now looking for the variables which represent the differential effect of culture on adjustment. As shown in Figure 7.3, the total variance accounted for, or R^2 (adjusted), for satisfaction with school when the cultural effects were partialled out was .23. If, however, we substitute the cultural means of the antecedent variables for the dichotomous variables representing our samples in the model, the amount of variance accounted for rises to 40% (see Figure 8.1). Note that the *betas* for the predictors in Figure 7.3 are identical to those in Figure 8.1 as we are merely substituting cultural means for the dichotomies used to control for sample differences.

Children will report higher satisfaction with school if they come from cultures who report lower family role differentiation based on sex and if the cultural mean for importance of friends is high. In addition to these cultural variables' direct effect on satisfaction with school, there was also an indirect effect for

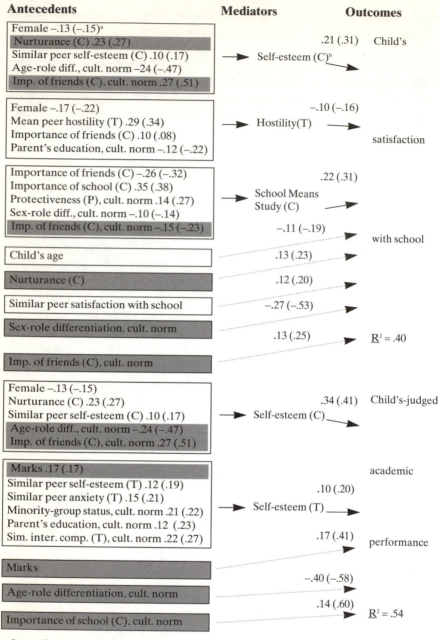

Antecedents	Mediators	Outcomes

Female –.13 (–.15)[a]
Nurturance (C) .23 (.27)
Similar peer self-esteem (C) .10 (.17)
Age-role diff., cult. norm –24 (–.47)
Imp. of friends (C). cult. norm .27 (.51)

.21 (.31)   Child's
Self-esteem (C)[b]

Female –.17 (–.22)
Mean peer hostility (T) .29 (.34)
Importance of friends (C) .10 (.08)
Parent's education, cult. norm –.12 (–.22)

–.10 (–.16)
Hostility(T)

satisfaction

Importance of friends (C) –.26 (–.32)
Importance of school (C) .35 (.38)
Protectiveness (P), cult. norm .14 (.27)
Sex-role diff., cult. norm –.10 (–.14)
Imp. of friends (C), cult. norm –.15 (–.23)

.22 (.31)
School Means
Study (C)

–.11 (–.19)   with school

Child's age

.13 (.23)

Nurturance (C)

.12 (.20)

Similar peer satisfaction with school

–.27 (–.53)

Sex-role differentiation, cult. norm

.13 (.25) R^2 = .40

Imp. of friends (C), cult. norm

Female –.13 (–.15)
Nurturance (C) .23 (.27)
Similar peer self-esteem (C) .10 (.17)
Age-role diff., cult. norm –.24 (–.47)
Imp. of friends (C), cult. norm .27 (.51)

.34 (.41)   Child's-judged
Self-esteem (C)

Marks .17 (.17)
Similar peer self-esteem (T) .12 (.19)
Similar peer anxiety (T) .15 (.21)
Minority-group status, cult. norm .21 (.22)
Parent's education, cult. norm .12 (.23)
Sim. inter. comp. (T), cult. norm .22 (.27)

academic

.10 (.20)
Self-esteem (T)

.17 (.41)   performance

Marks

Age-role differentiation, cult. norm

–.40 (–.58)

Importance of school (C), cult. norm

.14 (.60) R^2 = .54

[a] *Beta*-coefficients ≥ .10 only. Mean zero-order rs in brackets.

[b] Sources: C = Child; P = Parent; T = Teacher.

Note: Antecedents with direct and indirect effects are shaded. Hypothesized outcomes are represented by solid lines.

FIGURE 8.1   Direct and indirect cultural effects on subjective measures of academic adjustment.

importance of friends, which was partially mediated by school means study and the self-report on self-esteem. Family age-role differentiation's effect was also mediated by self-esteem; children from cultures whose families did not primarily assign roles by age or generation, reported higher satisfaction. And parental education, mediated by teacher-judged hostility, also was a determinant of school satisfaction. Remember that these cultural antecedents are in addition to the shared effect in all cultures of self-reported self-esteem and school means study, teacher-judged hostility, being young, having nurturant parents and having friends who are also satisfied with school. We can now say that children will be more satisfied with school if they come from cultures who, in comparison to others in our study, have low family sex-role and age-role differentiation and high importance of friends, in addition to the shared culture predictors.

Child-judged academic performance

The child's report of academic performance had a $\underline{R}^2$ (adjusted) of .23 with cultural effects partialled out (the sum of *beta* times the zero-order correlation for all predictors common to all seven samples). Over half the variance can be accounted for ($\underline{R}^2 = .54$) when the differences in cultural means for family age-role differentiation (*beta* = −.40) and importance of school (*beta* = .14) are entered into the model (Figure 8.1). Adding to the culturally shared predictors of high self-esteem (both child- and teacher-judged) and high marks, children judge themselves as performing better academically if they come from cultures with low family age-role differentiation and high importance of school scores.

Parent-judged academic performance

Figure 8.2 diagrams the predictors of parent's assessment of the child's academic performance. We find an augmentation of 14% when we take the specific cultural contributions into account. With culture partialled out, the $\underline{R}^2$ (adjusted) was .26. With the inclusion of the mean cultural scores of punitiveness (low), sex-role differentiation (low), and proportion of children being female added into the equation, it increases the overall $\underline{R}^2$ to .40. These cultural contributions are in addition to the culturally shared effect of low parental punitiveness (parent-judged), high child-judged self-esteem and high marks.

Teacher-judged academic performance

Finally, we examine the cultural effect on the teacher's ratings of academic performance (Figure 8.2), which already had 48% of the variance accounted for by knowing these same teacher's ratings of the child's self-esteem and (low) hostility plus the child's marks. Including the cultural mean of importance of friends added

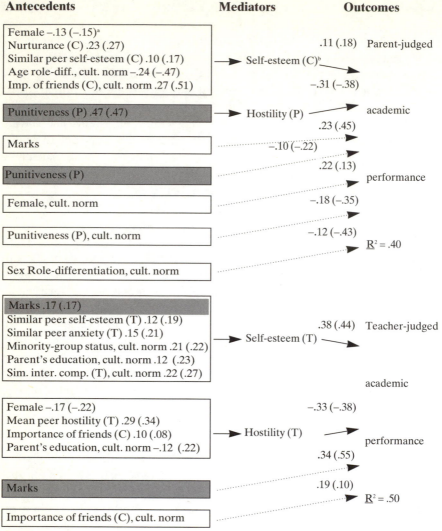

Antecedents	Mediators	Outcomes

FIGURE 8.2   Direct and indirect cultural effects on objective measures of academic adjustment.

only 2% to the accounted variance to reach an $\underline{R}^2$ of .50. Of course, most of this is due to the large halo effect of these teachers' ratings, for, as we saw in Chapter 2, when cross-source ratings were used to predict teacher's ratings of academic performance, the $\underline{R}^2$ dropped from .48 to .18 with culture partialled out (Table 2.3).

Summary

The importance of knowing the cultural norms when interpreting cross-cultural data is brought home by these results as the cultural norms for selected variables in the study did increase the predicability of the school adjustment scores, particularly for the child-judged measures. The cultural norms pertaining to the importance of friends had direct and indirect effects as mediated by school means study. The between-sample differences in proportion of females in the study also affected parent-judged academic performance directly, though it did not affect self-reported academic performance or reports from teachers. Lamborn, Dornbusch and Steinberg's (1996) observation of the effect on adolescents of increased decision-making responsibility at home leading to better adjustment is borne out by our results, through cultural norms, rather than a generalized finding across all samples. The less the culture's family roles are determined by the demographic characteristics of sex or age, the better adjusted the child. The implications of this will be touched upon in the last chapter.

Interpersonal adjustment

Satisfaction with friends

Inclusion of cultural norms in the regression equation for satisfaction with friends showed minimal effect, with only one with a *beta* $\geq$ .10, the child—peer similarity in interpersonal competence, as rated by the teacher. This increases the variance accounted for by 2% (Figure 8.3). Further, there is obviously something different about the Berlin measures of satisfaction and/or their predictors for which we have no measurable explanation as the unexplained variance attributed to Berlin has a *beta* weight of –.11, further increasing the $\underline{R}^2$ by .8%, bringing its total to .25. Indirectly, low cultural family age-role differentiation and high cultural importance of friends affect satisfaction with friends through self-esteem. Cultural norms on parental nurturance had an indirect effect, through anxiety. The mediators' self-esteem and (low) anxiety, along with the antecedents being female, having nurturant parents, having friends with similar satisfaction with friends, and feeling that friends are important, are all predictors of satisfaction with friends in all samples. Knowing about cultural differences did not add much to our understanding of this adjustment variable. We will discuss the implications of the unexplained variance attributed to Berlin and also the unexplained variance of the anxiety measure attributed to the Canberra sample when we discuss the differences in samples later in the chapter.

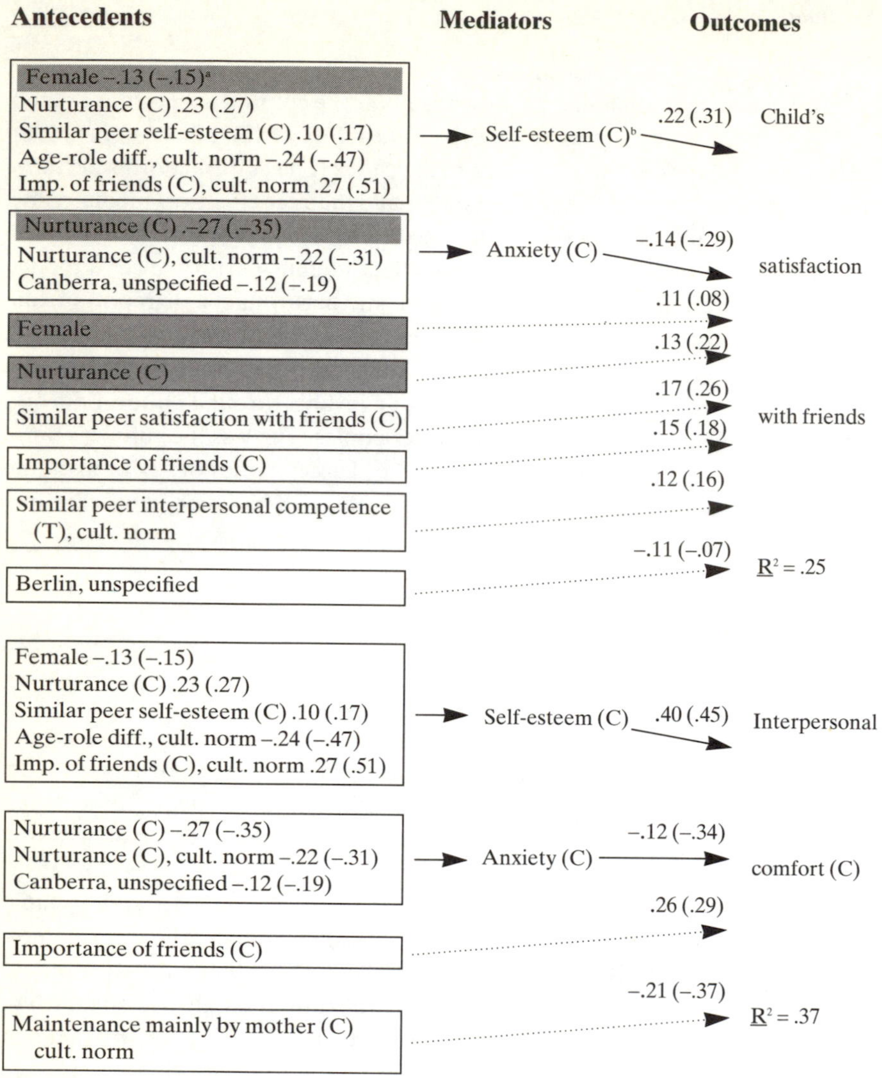

Antecedents	Mediators	Outcomes

Female −.13 (−.15)[a]
Nurturance (C) .23 (.27)
Similar peer self-esteem (C) .10 (.17)
Age-role diff., cult. norm −.24 (−.47)
Imp. of friends (C), cult. norm .27 (.51)

→ Self-esteem (C)[b] —— .22 (.31) Child's

Nurturance (C) .−27 (.−35)
Nurturance (C), cult. norm −.22 (−.31)
Canberra, unspecified −.12 (−.19)

→ Anxiety (C) —— −.14 (−.29) satisfaction

Female .... .11 (.08)

Nurturance (C) .... .13 (.22)

Similar peer satisfaction with friends (C) .... .17 (.26)

Importance of friends (C) .... .15 (.18) with friends

Similar peer interpersonal competence (T), cult. norm .... .12 (.16)

Berlin, unspecified .... −.11 (−.07) R² = .25

Female −.13 (−.15)
Nurturance (C) .23 (.27)
Similar peer self-esteem (C) .10 (.17)
Age-role diff., cult. norm −.24 (−.47)
Imp. of friends (C), cult. norm .27 (.51)

→ Self-esteem (C) —— .40 (.45) Interpersonal

Nurturance (C) −.27 (−.35)
Nurturance (C), cult. norm −.22 (−.31)
Canberra, unspecified −.12 (−.19)

→ Anxiety (C) —— −.12 (−.34) comfort (C)

Importance of friends (C) .... .26 (.29)

Maintenance mainly by mother (C) cult. norm .... −.21 (−.37) R² = .37

[a] *Beta*-coefficients ≥ .10 only. Mean zero-order rs in brackets.
[b] Sources: C = Child; T = Teacher.
Note: Antecedents with direct and indirect effects are shaded. Hypothesized outcomes are represented by solid lines.

FIGURE 8.3   Direct and indirect cultural effects on subjective measures of interpersonal adjustment.

Child's interpersonal comfort

The increase in the amount of variance accounted for in the child's report of interpersonal comfort (Figure 8.3) comes from including the cultural mean on the family having their maintenance functions performed mainly by the mother.

In cultures where this is the norm, the child is apt to report lower interpersonal comfort. This *beta* of –.21 leads to a 7% increase in the $\underline{R}^2$ to 37% of the variance accounted for when included along with the predictors found in all our cultures, the coping style variables self-esteem and anxiety plus the importance of friends.

Teacher-judged interpersonal competence

Figure 8.4 shows the model of teacher-judged interpersonal competence with the specific sample effect of importance of friends included. In addition, there were indirect effects from the cultural norms on migrant minority status, parent's education and similar interpersonal competence, teacher-judged, mediated by self-esteem (teacher-judged). The entry of the cultural mean on importance of friends increased the variance accounted for by a mere 1% to a total of 36% when

Antecedents	Mediators	Outcomes

Marks .17 (.17)
Similar peer self-esteem (T) .12 (.19)
Similar peer anxiety (T) .15 (.21)
Minority group status, cult. norm .21 (.22) → Self-esteem (T)[b]   .51 (.52)   Teacher-judged
Parent's education, cult. norm .12 (.23)
Sim. inter. comp. (T), cult. norm .22 (.27)   .23 (.33)   interpersonal

Similar peer interpersonal competence (T)   .15 (.13)   competence

Importance of friends (C), cult. norm $\underline{R}^2 = .36$

Female –.13 (–.15)
Nurturance (C) .23 (.27)
Similar peer self-esteem (C) .10 (.17) → Self-esteem (C)   .10 (.09)   Number of
Age-role diff., cult. norm –.24 (–.47)
Imp. of friends (C), cult. norm .27 (.51)   .28 (.24)

Mean peer sociometric status   .12 (.13)   friends chosen

Importance of friends (C)   –.10 (–.05)

Status mainly by father, cult. norm   .26 (.22)

Maintenance mainly by mother, cult. norm $\underline{R}^2 = .16$

Mean peer sociometric status   .27 (.23)   Sociometric

                                    .16 (.30)   status
Mean peer sociometric status, cult. norm $\underline{R}^2 = .11$

[a]   *Beta*-coefficients $\geq .10$ only. Mean zero-order $\underline{r}$s in brackets.

[b]   Sources: C = Child, T = Teacher.

Note. Antecedents with direct and indirect effects are shaded. Hypothesized outcomes are represented by solid lines.

FIGURE 8.4   Direct and indirect cultural effects on objective measures of interpersonal adjustment.

included with the culturally shared variables teacher-judged self-esteem and peer—child similarity in teacher-judged interpersonal competence.

Number of friends chosen

Our next indicator of interpersonal adjustment is the number of friends chosen to recreate with from the class (Figure 8.4). Up to now, the amount of variance accounted for by self-esteem, mean peer sociometric status and importance of friends in our combined sample with the effects of culture partialled out has been 10%. It is increased to the still low amount of 16% by the inclusion of cultural variables representing family status roles performed mainly by father (a negative effect) and maintenance roles performed mainly by mother (a positive effect). If the child is from a culture where the father is not the only one performing status roles, but the mother is the main performer of maintenance roles, then she/he is more likely to choose many friends to recreate with.

Sociometric status

The sociometric rating received by our children has, in essence, no predictors other than that those who are chosen most select peers as friends who also are "stars" (Figure 8.4). This extends to cultural effects, also, in that cultures also differ on the clustering of sociometric choices, with some cultures showing greater concentration of choices. The predicted variance is now 11%, up from only 6% when cultural differences on peer sociometric status were not taken into account.

Summary

The subjective interpersonal adjustment measure, satisfaction with friends, showed little effect from cultural norms. For both subjective measures of interpersonal adjustment, cultures with low parental nurturance influence these outcome measures indirectly by being associated with high anxiety. In addition, the more objective self-report measure of interpersonal comfort was influenced by the cultural norm relating to mothers being the main provider of maintenance, the children in those cultures having lower interpersonal comfort scores. Perhaps experience in family maintenance roles leads to better preparation in taking on interpersonal roles in a wider setting.

When we turn to teacher-judged interpersonal competence, the cultural effect was, again, minor. Teachers do rate children as more competent if the cultural norms indicate relatively higher ranking of importance of friends. Number of friends chosen seems to be higher in cultures where the father is not the only provider of status roles yet the mother is the main provider of maintenance roles. Finally, sociometric status reflects the fact that popular children nominate stars in cultures where choosing stars is valued and make idiosyncratic choices in cultures where choosing on a basis other than class popularity is the norm. Overall, in contrast to academic adjustment measures, the culture in which one is imbedded seems to have less effect on the level of interpersonal adjustment.

Family adjustment

Child's satisfaction with family

Looking first at the child's report on family satisfaction as one measure of family adjustment, we see that there is a high proportion of variance accounted for when just self-esteem and parental nurturance, the two predictors found in all seven cultures, is taken into account. The R^2 increased minimally from .43 to .44 when the cultural variable family status roles performed mainly by father is included (see Figure 8.5).

Parent's satisfaction with family

In contrast, the cultural mean difference in parental education and proportion of minority groups in the sample does seem to have an effect on both parent's family satisfaction and parent's satisfaction with the child's behaviour, with parents from cultures whose average education level is relatively high and who have a higher proportion of respondents having minority group status being more satisfied with their families and children. These are the only two cultural variables affecting parent's satisfaction with family and raises the variance accounted for from 23% to 30% (Figure 8.5).

Satisfaction with child's behaviour

For parental satisfaction with child's behaviour, we find that there is a further increase when the variable representing the cultural norm for the proportion of family maintenance roles performed by mothers is included. In those cultures who report more shared maintenance functions, the mothers report higher satisfaction with their child's behaviour. And, finally, in the cultures with high importance of friends' mean scores, parents also see the child's behaviour in a more favourable light (Figure 8.5). To the results obtained on the analysis based on common predictors across all seven samples, there is an increase to the explained variance from 21% to 38% for this outcome variable. Though family adjustment as viewed through the eyes of the child, seems relatively uninfluenced by cultural norms, the parent's evaluation of the family does seem to be determined in part by its culture.

Antecedents	Mediators	Outcomes

Female −.13 (−.15)[a]
Nurturance (C) .23 (.27)
Similar peer self-esteem (C) .10 (.17)
Age-role diff., cult. norm −.24 (−.47)
Imp. of Friends (C), cult. norm .27 (.51)

→ Self-esteem (C)[b] → .19 (.31) Child's

satisfaction

Nurturance (C) .... .59 (.62) → with family

Status mainly by father, cult. norm .... .12 (.09) → $\underline{R}^2 = .44$

−.30 (−.38)

Punitiveness (P) .47 (.47) → Hostility (P) → Parent's
.18 (.24)

Nurturance (C) .... .22 (.33) → satisfaction

Similar peer family satisfaction (P) .... .20 (.25) → with family

Parent's education, cult. norm .... .16 (.15) →

Minority-group status, cult. norm .... → $\underline{R}^2 = .30$

−.33 (−.42) Satisfaction

Punitiveness (P) .47 (.47) → Hostility (P) →

Nurturance (C) .... .13 (.24) →

Protectiveness (P) .... −.17 (−.23) → with child's

Parent's education, cult. norm .... .16 (.39) →

Minority-group status, cult. norm .... .14 (.25) → behaviour (P)
−.12 (−.35)

Maintenance mainly by mother, cult. norm .... →

Importance of friends (C), cult. norm .... .12 (.28) → $\underline{R}^2 = .38$

[a] *Beta*-coefficients $\geq$ .10 only. Mean zero-order $\underline{r}$s in brackets.

[b] Sources: C = Child; P = Parent.

Note: Antecedents with direct and indirect effects are shaded. Hypothesized outcomes represented by solid lines.

FIGURE 8.5   Direct and indirect cultural effects on family adjustment.

Relative Effect of Cultural Differences: Summary

Shortly, we will be addressing the cultural differences in these results as they apply to our seven samples, but let's first take an overall view of the findings. The increase in $\underline{R}^2$ obtained from the combined sample with the mean culture value entered into the equation, along with the dummy sample variables, is summarized in Figure 8.6. For each dependent measure of adjustment, the proportion of variance accounted for by the substantive predictors combined into domains is entered; first, the mediators, personality and meaning of school, followed by the unmediated demographic variables as discussed in Chapter 4, then the family (Chapter 6), peer and attitude (Chapter 7) antecedents. Finally, we add on the proportion contributed by the different cultures included in this study. This final augmentation to the R^2 is represented in two ways: by the culture mean of known (measured) variables, and the unattributed contribution from a specific culture which was either not assessed in this study or is due to measurement error.

There is a direct effect from cultural differences on all 12 adjustment measures, though the percentage varies from 1%, for the child's satisfaction with family, to 31% for the child's report on his/her own academic performance. Indirect effects of culture are through all mediators except hostility which still has only one predictor, punitiveness, and raises the issue of whether or not we have adequately distinguished the concepts. For almost all cultural contributions we have been able to isolate the source of the cultural differences to specific variables; the exception being the non-specific direct contribution to satisfaction with friends and the indirect effect through the mediator anxiety.

Overall, we seem to know most about academic adjustment with a range of 40 to 54% of the variance accounted for in measures from children, parents and teachers. We know least about interpersonal adjustment. This may in part be due to the fact that choices of friends had to be limited to those in the classroom, which is a restricted sample of friendships and types of interaction. The unaccounted cultural variance from our measure of satisfaction with friends and the mediator most affecting interpersonal relations, anxiety, also suggests problems with measurement, as we have between-sample variance unaccounted for by content. Finally, adjustment of families seems to lie between these two areas of adjustment as far as predicability goes, with between 30% and 44% of variance accounted for. We will come back to the influence of the family role variables, representing that which is the norm for the cultural community, as we discuss the adjustment differences in our samples.

Inter-Cultural Similarities

Cross-cultural research has, over the past half century, been concerned not so much with the similarities of relationship between variables over cultures, but with differences. Yet when comparing only two cultures, the degrees of freedom are zero. While the discovery of inter-cultural differences and their bases is, for many, the principal goal of cross-cultural psychology, an equally important and potentially more attainable goal is the establishment of inter-cultural similarities. Useful steps toward this objective can be taken with a smaller sample of cultures

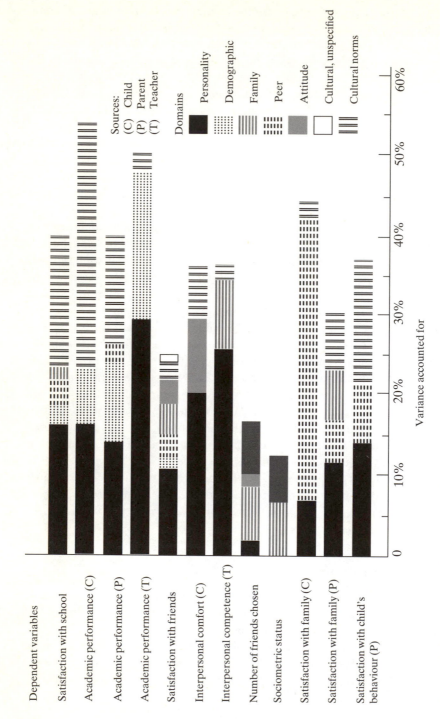

FIGURE 8.6 Percentage of variance accounted for by domain, each adjustment variable separately.

if one views different cultures as different treatments in a treatment-by-measures design (Strodtbeck, 1964).

The main problem lies in defining the criteria for similarity. As the reader knows, it is much more logical to reject than to accept a null hypothesis (of no difference) on the basis of data obtained from several samples. In the comparison of means from large samples, F-tests typically yield large values, which subsequently leads to the conclusion that one culture differs significantly from another on a particular variable. In fact, it is surprising to find non-significant Fs on most variables of a study.

Comparison of product-moment rs among several samples is another matter. It is rather rare to find overall significant differences among rs. Although a particular culture may turn out to be different from the others, isolated differences, discovered *ex post facto*, are not dependable. Just as unpredicted differences among means need to be validated by an overall F test of significance, so unpredicted differences among rs need to be validated by some overall test before any one of them can be taken seriously. The test we chose for this purpose was an F-ratio between the obtained variance among rs over the seven samples and the variance that would be expected by chance, given the average sample size (computed as the harmonic mean of the sample sizes).

Applying this procedure to the statistics on agreement between parents and children in the seven cultures on two aspects of children's personality (anxiety and hostility) and four aspects of family relations (family satisfaction, parental nurturance, parental protectiveness and parental punitiveness), we found no F-ratios significant at the .05 level. This means that the levels of inter-source agreement were remarkably similar in the seven samples. Moreover, the 48 correlations between family characteristics and children's personalities from same and different sources showed no significant Fs across cultures (at $p < .05$). So the relationships found in this study were virtually the same from sample to sample. This is not to say that inter-cultural differences in rs did not exist, but in order to depend on them, one would need some a priori hypotheses that allowed a more powerful test of significance than the F-test did.

Inter-Cultural Differences

When cross-cultural correlations between predictors and dependent variables mirror within-cultural rs, they offer us a chance to interpret cultural differences. As an example, the cross-cultural r between the seven mean family satisfaction scores as predicted by the parent is correlated .91 with the seven mean child's self-report scores of self-esteem. The mean within culture r for these same variables is .23, both highly significant. The main conclusion to be drawn from these results is that the variables of interest were comparably measured within the seven samples, as represented by the mean within-culture r of .23. Therefore, a cross-cultural comparison of those scores (r = .91) is interpretable: cultures whose children score high on self-esteem have higher reports of family satisfaction just as school children within each culture who are high on self-esteem also report high family-satisfaction.

To facilitate cross-cultural comparisons of our results, each of the scores was standardized to the mean and standard deviation of the composite sample. The zero-points are arbitrary—simply the means from the composite sample. Within each sample, comparisons among the adjustment scores are not meaningful as they consist of different components. But between samples, means can be compared on a given variable, and many of the mean differences are reliable. Here we will summarize the inter-cultural differences for our three major areas of adjustment, academic, inter-personal and family, along with the major antecedent variables which help interpret the sample differences in the mediators and adjustment scores. Table 8.1 presents the mean cultural z-scores (see Table 2.1 for the ns) for these variables and we will be referring to this table as we discuss the cultural differences in our outcome variables. But, we will start with a look at the differences in coping styles among our seven samples and how the differences among them in mean antecedent scores can help in understanding them.

The mediators

The z-scores for the six variables which we predict mediate the antecedent effects on adjustment are presented in Figure 8.7, with the sample similarities, based on Newman-Keuls, represented by common letters. Similar patterns emerge in their relative rankings with English language and Berlin cultures higher on self-esteem, child- or teacher-assessed, and lower on anxiety than the Oriental cultures. The importance of parental nurturance for understanding low anxiety scores which we found within each sample, is reflected in the parallel ranking of their cultural mean scores. Likewise, the effect of low age and sex-role differentiation in families on self-reported self-esteem of the child is reflected in the similar pattern in their means. Not surprisingly, the z-score for parent-judged hostility reflects the same pattern as that of its only antecedent, parent-judged punitiveness; Osaka is much higher than all the other samples, which are indistinguishable (see Table 8.1). In contrast, teacher-judged hostility shows Berlin with significantly higher average scores than Hong Kong and Osaka, with Taipei and the English-language cultures very similar. Finally, Taipei's mean is much higher on school means study than the English-language cultures, who are, in turn, higher than Berlin and Hong Kong. Osaka has the lowest average for this variable.

There are also demographic differences in the samples, probably due to different recruitment procedures of participants; these included the education level of the responding parent and the proportion of minorities in the sample. And they

TABLE 8.1 Mean culture z-scores for major independent variables

	Hong Kong	Taipei	Osaka	Berlin	Winnipeg	Phoenix	Canberra
Demographics							
Age (C)*	0.45**[a]	-0.06[c]	0.14[c]	-0.10[c]	-0.61[c]	-0.01[c]	-0.37[d]
Female (C)	-0.07[b]	-0.15[c]	0.09[b]	-0.31[d]	0.09[abc]	0.31[a]	0.06[b]
Marks		0.43[a]		-0.81[c]	0.40[a]	-0.46[b]	0.21[a]
Parental education	-1.02[d]	-0.10[b]	-0.44[c]	-0.44[c]	0.32[a]	0.43[a]	0.3[a]
Minority-group status	0.35[a]	-0.20[b]		-0.04[b]	0.35[a]	-0.18[b]	0.34[a]
Family							
Parental practices							
Nurturance (C)	-0.58[a]	-0.07[b]	-0.08[a]	0.39[a]	0.38[a]	0.24[a]	0.37[a]
Protectiveness (P)	0.62[b]	0.95[a]	-0.03[c]	-0.89[f]	-0.90[ef]	-0.70[e]	-0.57[d]
Punitiveness (P)	0.04[b]	-0.08[bc]	0.51[a]	-0.30[c]	-0.06[bc]	-0.01[bc]	-0.25[b]
Family Roles							
Sex-role differentiation (C)	0.48[b]	-0.04[c]	0.66[a]	-0.29[d]	-0.42[e]	-0.30[d]	-0.57[e]
Age-role differentiation (C)	0.13[b]	0.23[b]	0.30[a]	-0.30[c]	-0.14[c]	-0.33[c]	-0.19[c]
Status by father (C)	-0.16[c]	0.37[a]	-0.08[bc]	-0.10[bc]	-0.10[bc]	-0.19[c]	0.04[b]
Maint. by mother (C)	-0.03[b]	0.04[b]	0.69[a]	0.08[b]	-0.24[c]	-0.37[c]	-0.26[c]
Peers							
Peer similarity							
Similar self-esteem (C)	0.00	-0.01	0.08	0.15	-0.22	-0.09	0.03
Similar self-esteem (T)	-0.08[b]	-0.11[b]	0.24[a]	-0.07[b]	-0.34[b]	-0.04[b]	0.27[a]
Similar school satisfaction	0.03[a]	0.02[a]	0.05[a]	0.05[a]	-0.33[b]	-0.21[b]	0.21[a]
Similar friend satisfaction	0.08[a]	0.05[a]	-0.10[ab]	0.08[a]	0.04[ab]	-0.20[b]	0.09[a]
Similar interpersonal competence (T)	-0.16[bc]	0.19[a]	0.02[b]	-0.21[c]	-0.17[bc]	-0.26[c]	0.34[a]
Similar family satisfaction (P)	-0.32[c]	0.13[a]	-0.03[abc]	0.18[ab]	-0.24[abc]	-0.14[bc]	-0.01[abc]
Mean Peer Scores							
Mean peer hostility (T)	0.31[b]	-0.34[d]	0.22[b]	1.08[a]	-0.15[cd]	-0.41[d]	-0.01[c]
Peer sociometric status	-0.66[f]	-0.04[d]	-0.19[c]	0.93[a]	1.06[a]	0.38[b]	0.12[c]
Attitudes							
Importance of school (C)	-0.69[f]	0.01[d]	-0.40[c]	0.24[c]	0.66[a]	0.44[ab]	0.44[ab]
Importance of friends (C)	-0.40[d]	-0.45[d]	0.40[ab]	0.17[c]	0.09[c]	0.39[a]	0.24[bc]

* C = Child's report; P = Parent's report; T = Teacher's report.
** z-scores with identical letters are not significantly different, p < .05, using Newman-Keuls. See Table 2.1 for sample ns.

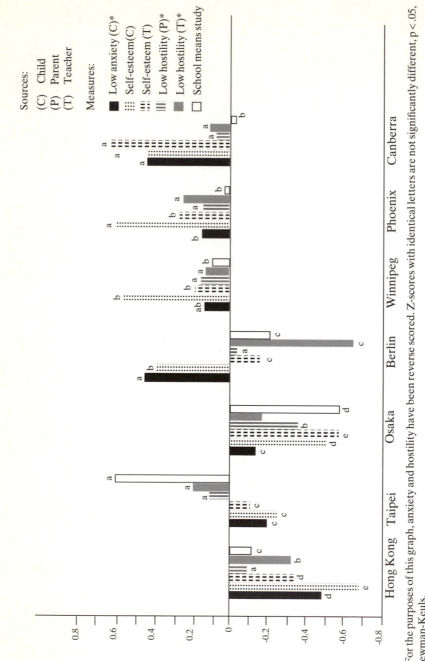

Sources:

(C) Child
(P) Parent
(T) Teacher

Measures:

■ Low anxiety (C)*
▦ Self-esteem(C)
▤ Self-esteem (T)
▥ Low hostility (P)*
▨ Low hostility (T)*
□ School means study

Note: *For the purposes of this graph, anxiety and hostility have been reverse scored. Z-scores with identical letters are not significantly different, p < .05, using Newman-Keuls.

FIGURE 8.7   Cultural z-scores for mediators.

did affect teachers' ratings of both the child's self-esteem and hostility. Though these and other differential effects of cultural norms affected all mediators, not all result in a parallel between the ranks of antecedents and the ranks of the coping styles. But, in the areas in which past research leads one to expect cultural effects, there is a parallel: self-esteem and (low) anxiety are high in samples which are also high on parental nurturance (Steinberg, Elmen and Mounts, 1989); and family age-role differential is low in samples which are high on self-esteem as found by Lamborn, Dornbusch and Steinberg (1996).

The dependent variables

Academic adjustment

Figure 8.8 presents the four academic adjustment measures transformed into z-scores for the seven cultures and Table 8.1 shows the z-scores for both direct and indirect cultural antecedents of these same adjustment measures. For all four measures of academic adjustment, regardless of source, Canberra, Phoenix and Winnipeg were significantly higher than Berlin and the three Oriental cultures using the Newman-Kuels test for group order. These results, as with self-reported self-esteem, demonstrate the importance of parental nurturance as a precursor to satisfaction with school; cultures high on this antecedent are also high on the outcome variable.

Though the ordering of means for the proportion of females and importance of school are as expected, as they reflect cultural rankings on the academic performance measures (English-language cultures higher than Oriental), the fact that the Berlin sample had a lower proportion of males participating may be a contribution to its lower ranking in academic adjustment as males have higher self-esteem, one of the major predictors. In contrast, school means study shows Osaka ranking the lowest (see Figure 8.7), even though it ranks the highest on academic performance (Figure 8.8). Students in Osaka who rank their academic performance high, are doing so in a culture which, as a whole, ranks school means study lower (and, as it is a bimodel scale, school means friends higher) than one would expect from the composite sample. This may have to do with the streaming of schools in Japan. Once one has been accepted at a particular level of school, the main emphasis at school is the contacts one makes (in contrast to actual exam preparation), hence the high ranking given to the importance of friends (see Table 8.1) in contrast to the low ranking given to importance of school in the Osaka school culture.

Now to the effect of cultural differences in family practices on academic performance for our samples. Firstly, the samples with low parental punitiveness (e.g. Osaka), as reported by the parent, seem also to have the child reporting lower academic adjustment (also Osaka). Further, over-protective cultures, Taipei in our study, contribute to higher school-means-study orientation and thus

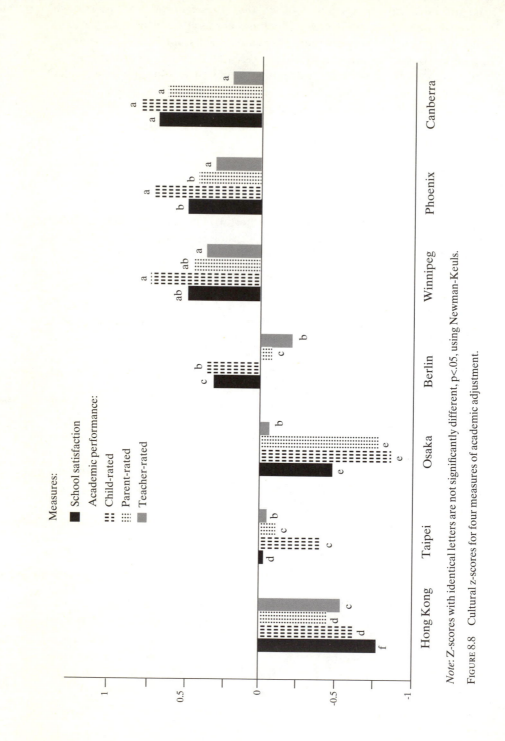

Note: Z-scores with identical letters are not significantly different, p<.05, using Newman-Keuls.

FIGURE 8.8   Cultural z-scores for four measures of academic adjustment.

to higher satisfaction with school. This later result may reflect the Taipei orientation of family involvement in the importance of studying at school. The effect of cultural differences in family structure on these measures of academic adjustment is exciting. Cultures whose families have roles filled using criteria of other than age or sex, from the Occidental samples, have children who are judged by others and who report themselves to have higher academic adjustment. The Oriental samples, in which there are more traditional role assignments, i.e. father or mother who make decisions, mothers who performed all maintenance roles, have children who are less satisfied. In addition, low cultural age-role differentiation scores not only has a direct effect on academic adjustment, but also an indirect effect through its negative relationship with the child's self-esteem. Once again, this finding supports the interpretation of Lamborn, Dornbusch and Steinberg (1996) that older children do better as they take on more adult roles in the family.

In conclusion, the type of family structure and the relative value placed on friends and school in the samples being examined did affect the level of academic adjustment.

Interpersonal adjustment

We turn now to the effect of culture on interpersonal adjustment. Overall, the three measures of interpersonal adjustment reflecting satisfaction with friends and subjective and objective interpersonal competence (see Figure 8.9) show the same pattern as the academic adjustment measures with the highest adjustment scores in the English-language cultures, the Oriental with the lowest, and Berlin, once again in between. This pattern also holds for another objective interpersonal measure, the child's sociometric status. When we examine the relative cross-cultural norms for number of friends chosen, the highest number selected is by Osaka children and the lowest by those of Hong Kong, Taipei, Canberra and Phoenix. As the total amount of variance accounted for is very low for both sociometric status and number of friends chosen, it seems risky to make too much of their cultural predictors. As we have mentioned before, this is probably a function of the limitation of friends to those in the class, as this did not allow for an adequate representation of the child's friends as contrasted to peers, and, therefore, not a precise enough operational definition of interpersonal adjustment.

Also, it is in this domain of adjustment that we have evidence of inadequate coverage of possible antecedents of interpersonal adjustment, specifically satisfaction with friends and its mediator, anxiety, with unspecified variance attributed to the Canberra sample for anxiety and to the Berlin sample for satisfaction with friends. This may have to do with either the conceptualization or the measurement of anxiety and/or its predictors. Whereas the Berlin mean was the lowest along with a next-to-lowest score on satisfaction-with-friends, in Canberra the mean satisfaction-with-friends was the highest and anxiety the lowest, and in

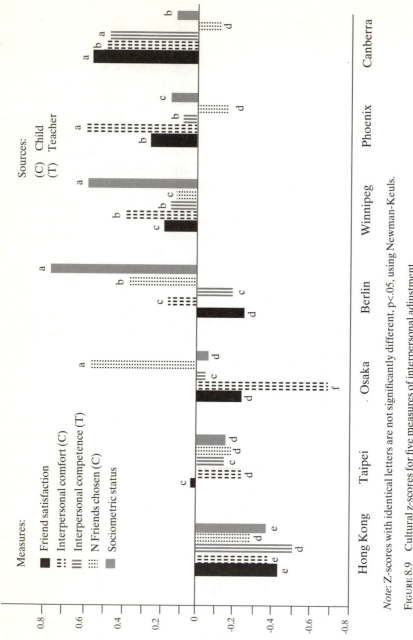

Measures:

■ Friend satisfaction
⋮⋮ Interpersonal comfort (C)
▦ Interpersonal competence (T)
⋮⋮ N Friends chosen (C)
▨ Sociometric status

Sources:
(C) Child
(T) Teacher

Hong Kong   Taipei   Osaka   Berlin   Winnipeg   Phoenix   Canberra

Note: Z-scores with identical letters are not significantly different, p<.05, using Newman-Keuls.

FIGURE 8.9   Cultural z-scores for five measures of interpersonal adjustment.

Hong Kong, the mean satisfaction-with-friends score was the lowest and anxiety the highest (a more expected result).

In conclusion, interpersonal adjustment gives a much less clear picture of the effects of demographic, family, peer and culture on adjustment than do the academic adjustment antecedents. Given these limitations, we can still point to the effect of importance of cultural variation in family structure and practices as antecedents to adjustment with the positive effect of egalitarian role distribution mediated by self-esteem in the Occidental cultures, and in these same cultures, those with higher parental nurturance in their families showing children with lower anxiety, leading to higher satisfaction with friends and higher self-reported interpersonal comfort.

Family adjustment

Turning to the three family adjustment measures (Figure 8.10), we again see the three English-language cultures significantly higher on adjustment than the Oriental for both measures based on parent's ratings, with Berlin between the two when using parental satisfaction with child's behaviour and indistinguishable from Taipei though still significantly higher than Hong Kong and Osaka when examining parental satisfaction with family. The picture is different when looking at child's satisfaction with family. Hong Kong is still lowest, but Taipei is the highest, though indistinguishable from Canberra and Winnipeg, with Phoenix in the middle, indistinguishable from Osaka and Berlin. Once more, the pattern of sample means reflects the same differences found in self-esteem, and, for the area of parental satisfaction with the family and child's behaviour, parents judgment of low hostility (see Figure 8.7).

Though the cultural effect on satisfaction with family is minimal, for parents the cultural context is quite important. The Hong Kong school had the least-educated parent respondents and this sample also shows parents less satisfied with the family in general and the child's behaviour more specifically. With the exception of Hong Kong, a high proportion of minority-group-status families in the sample is seen to promote higher family satisfaction responses for parents. We suspect that the Hong Kong "mainlanders" should not have been coded as minority-group members, which would have left Hong Kong without minority-group representation, and their results more in line with Osaka's, who also had no minority-group members, namely showing an association between cultural homogeneity and low parental family satisfaction.

Summary

When we look at mean cultural z-scores, of primary importance is the consistency in the ordering of the samples across the dependent variables and their

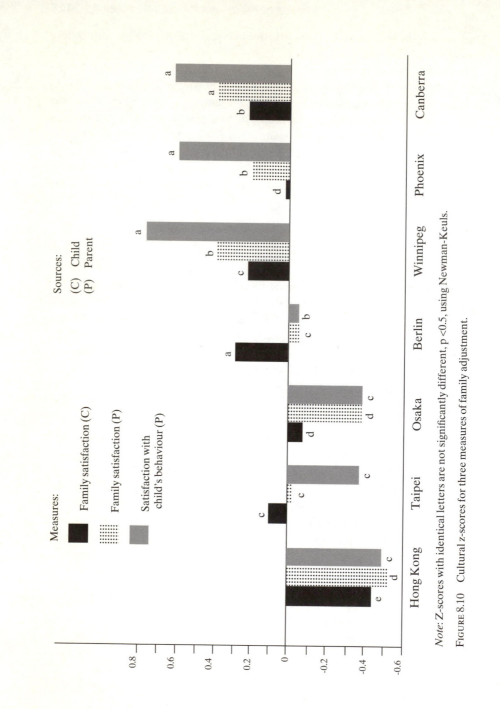

Note: Z-scores with identical letters are not significantly different, p <0.5, using Newman-Keuls.

FIGURE 8.10 Cultural z-scores for three measures of family adjustment.

predictors, be they antecedents or mediators; and as reported by divergent sources, the child, parent or teacher. The usual ranking of the 12 measures of adjustment across cultures finds the English-language cultures the highest, Berlin the least consistent, and the three Oriental cultures the lowest. These between-sample comparisons mirror the results from our within-sample analyses, which showed that adolescents within each culture who are high on self-esteem, (either child or teacher rated) and high on parental nurturance, are high on adjustment. Osaka deviated from this order in their ratings of friends as more important than even Hong Kong or Taipei. The mediation of this by school means study is reflected in the Osaka students' very low rating of that variable and on the academic adjustment measures affected by that, e.g. satisfaction with school and self-report on academic performance (both low).

Including the cultural means of antecedents did increase the predicability of the subjective academic adjustment measure of satisfaction, and the more objective measures of academic performance as judged by the child. In contrast, satisfaction with friends showed little influence from cultural norms, though in the samples where mothers did not perform all the maintenance roles for the family, there was an increase also in self-report of interpersonal comfort. Finally, though there is remarkably little effect from the cultural norms we measured on child-judged family adjustment, the cultural level of education did lead to increased academic performance scores from the teachers.

In support of our hypotheses, there were cultural effects, from family variables on our mediators, which, in turn, affected adjustment. Of primary interest, cultures with norms encouraging adolescents to participate in family decisions, those with low mean age-role and sex-role differentiation scores, also reported higher adjustment levels. Further, the assessment of low anxiety is influenced by high parental nurturance in cultures with low norms. Finally, the generality of the concept hostility from one sample to another is notable, with only the teacher showing any influence from differing cultural norms on any measured variable, that of low parental education.

As these constitute only a minute sample of world cultures, it is hazardous to draw conclusions about cross-cultural differences in the world at large. Nevertheless, it is worth noting that the cross-cultural differences are, for the most part, exaggerated mirrors of within-cultural relations (r=.74 p < .01). In general, parental nurturance fosters children's adjustment — especially nurturance as seen by the children; parental protectiveness and punitiveness impede school and family adjustment.

When cross-cultural relations parallel within-cultural relations, it seems logical to apply the same rationale to their bases as to the within-cultural results: nurturance, from the child's perspective, favours good adjustment, while protectiveness and punitiveness impede it. Cultures in which children regard their parents as generally nurturant tend to produce children with higher self-esteem, which, in turn, is associated with higher subjective and objective academic and interpersonal adjustment scores than non-nurturant cultures. Further, cultures which reflect exposing adolescents to decision making and role sharing in families (low age- and sex-role differentiation), also contribute to increased adjustment either directly or indirectly, through their effect on self-esteem; and cultures where mothers are mainly responsible for family maintenance may not allow the child enough experience to result in his/her feeling comfortable in other interpersonal situations.

9

Summaries and Conclusions

In the present era of quick, single-focus research, it seems appropriate to remind others of the gains achieved by instigating, carrying out and publishing research using complex data from more than one source and multiple predictors from more than one domain when building models for predicting behaviour. We have gone into our methodology in some detail as we feel it is inexorably intertwined with the substance of a study. We have used seven culturally diverse samples, four sources of information, three adjustment areas, and predictive variables from several content domains. This parallels closely Jessor's (1993) requirements for a developmental behavioural science based on multidisciplinary approaches, akin to our domains of antecedents (demographics, family, peers and culture); and data based on internal experiences and overt behaviour, which we called subjective and objective sources of information. We were led to pick adolescents as the focus of study as human maturation requires adaptation to changing roles in multiple areas of life at puberty, irrespective of culture. Of course, other equally stressful events requiring adaptation to more than one role in life could have been selected as the focus of this cross-cultural study, such as birth of the first child, leaving home or migrating.

Theoretical Overview

This study has looked at adolescent adjustment as a multifaceted process by which the overall coping mechanisms, as represented by personality and general orientation and influenced by demographics and the social context in which they are embedded (family, classmates and culture), determine adaptation to particular situations. Note that we do not assume a general adaptability to all situations, but rather a specificity depending on the demands of the particular situation which have their own predictors. More specifically, we proposed that:

1. Adjustment to specific situations (academic, interpersonal or family) will be mediated by an overall predisposition to appropriate coping behaviour.
2. The situation-specific adjustment measure will be affected by the judgemental source, though there will be a positive relationship between them.

3.   Subjective and objective adjustment measures, with source and situation constant, will depend on different predictors; this will result in lower agreement among variables within the same domain.
4.   The social environment information, including that about the culture itself, will increase the ability to predict the level of adjustment.

Methodical Contributions

The adjustment models developed here were based on findings replicated in seven different cultures. Obviously, the directions of effect are dictated from theory, rather than unequivocally demonstrated by the pattern of correlations and *beta*-coefficients from these cross-sectional results. It is possible, for instance, that high self-esteem, low hostility, and emphasis on scholarship are consequences, rather than determinants, of school satisfaction, but this awaits more searching, longitudinal studies.

To interpret our data, multiple-regression analyses were performed with between-sample differences partialled out, to construct models which could describe the effects of various domains of variables, either as mediated by the students' coping mechanisms or directly onto the adjustment measures which would be applicable in all seven samples. Overall, within-sample correlations among the variables were similar (within the bounds of random sampling error) yielding models very similar across samples. Where there were between-sample differences, an attempt was made to determine the specific antecedent variables on which they differed. Including these variables led to further increases in the amount of variance explained in adjustment measures. These were discussed in Chapter 8, when we summarized the overall models in respect to cultural similarities and differences. The identification of these future variables also points to potentially profitable areas for future research, which, hopefully, will lead to a more complete understanding of the antecedents of successful adjustment.

The samples

Questionnaires were presented in the language of the participating cultures: Cantonese, English, German, Japanese and Mandarin. All students were from urban schools in industrialized societies, and all respondents (including parents) were literate. Selection methods ranged from stratified (by academic achievement) random sampling of schools and classes to volunteers from classes whose participation was determined by teacher interest. The response rate differed markedly across our samples, with almost full participation in Oriental cultures to only volunteers in the Occidental ones. This could be a factor in the higher scores on self-esteem and lower scores on anxiety, and, therefore, higher adjustment scores, from those samples with low participation rates. These differences in sample characteristics could also have limited particularly the impact the data from friends had, as these data were limited to those who also responded in the classroom. One can only speculate on what new insights will emerge when schools from the non-industrialized third world are included and when truly random samples from a sample of cultures is obtained (see Feldman and Elliott, 1990).

The sources of data

Our data were sought from more than one source: the child, a parent, a teacher, classmates and cultural norms. All the independent variables from the same source may reflect a general overall view of the world; an outside observer might report on them more selectively. For instance, though high parental nurturance and low parental punitiveness and over-protectiveness correlate highly with overall family satisfaction when all data come from the same source, when the independent variables of parental practices comes from a different rater, though the association remains high, the predictors were more differentiated in their effect. However, just as subjective ratings of both dependent and independent variables have "error" contributed by non-objectivity, so, too, do objective reports; their error as a result of ignorance about relevant data or bias in interpretation by the outsider as a result of the outsider's own characteristics.

The measures

Our measures of adjustment were quite uniform in reliability and validity over the seven samples, indicating that cross-culturally comparable measures had been developed. The highest mean item agreement for our cultures occurred for the child's self-reported and parent-judged academic performance, child's and parent's satisfaction with family, child-reported parental nurturance and parent-reported protectiveness (all .90 or higher). For these scales, the variables yielded similar relative scores for the seven cultures; that is, the cross-cultural differences are reliable. The lower homogeneity ratios appeared for the scales of anxiety, hostility, teacher-judged interpersonal competence and the child's satisfaction with friends, which implies that the cross-cultural comparisons are suspect, for different ways of measuring the variables did not yield the same results. This is borne out by the fact that there was unspecified variance attributed to sample differences (in contrast to differences in antecedent norms) for both anxiety and satisfaction with friends.

The choice of variables to represent our domains of concern was theory-driven with the objective of providing replication of (mostly) Occidental or Western (predominantly American) results. In addition, variables representing alternative or ambient theories for interpreting the consequences of the selected antecedents of adjustment were also included. Adjustment measures were based both on the work of previous investigators and on those developed uniquely for this study.

The impact of type of measurement employed on outcome variables is always a matter for concern; especially when there may be differential effects of various segments on the sample under study. Cross-cultural research is a prime example. Chen, Lee and Stevenson (1995) have shown a relationship between the respondents' ratings on individualism and collectivism and their use of extreme versus moderate ratings on scales used to ascertain their positions on seven multi-item scales involving the respondents' attitudes and values. Those high on individualism were more likely to use the scale extremes, those high on collectivism, the moderate range when responding to the scale items. Leung and Bond (1989) support the notion that those from more interdependent societies (Hong Kong, Taipei and Osaka in our study) wish *not* to stand out, therefore present a more moderate view of themselves.

Markus and Kitayama (1991) found these differences between Asian and Western cultures; Asian participants and their mothers' rating ability lower and less positive personality characteristics higher than in their Western counterparts. Our data reflect this also, and, as our cultures could certainly be expected to differ on the individualism—interdependence dimension, interpreting mean cultural differences must be done cautiously. Furthermore, as we did not sample from all possible variables about which data could have been obtained, we are reluctant to make too much of cultural differences except when they parallel intra-sample results (etic analysis) or when there are strong theoretical rationales to support the interpretation of results. However, cultural differences can be important signposts for future avenues of research as we continue to expand our understanding of the factors influencing adjustment.

The Final Models: A Summary

The general hypotheses were examined with respect to the child's adjustment to school, friends and family, measured subjectively (self-report), and objectively, as evaluated by role partners (parent, teacher and peer). The impact of family, peer and culture were hypothesized to be through the coping characteristics: self-esteem, anxiety, hostility and orientation towards school. These were predicted to mediate the effects of our antecedent variables comprising demographic data on both students and their responding parent, information on family relations including family roles and their allocation, parental practices (nurturance, protectiveness and punitiveness), measures of peer influence, (peer mean and the similarity of child and mean peer), and, lastly, the effect of cultural norms. Though we had predicted that these effects would be mediated by their ability to cope, we, in fact, did find some direct effects. Generally, there was uniformity over cultures in magnitude of the correlations, but, in a study encompassing seven sample points in seven different cultures, there were some differential effects among them. Overall, Oriental samples score lower than English-language cultures on most situation-specific adjustment scores, regardless of source. They also scored lower on measures of coping, reflected most notably in the mediating variable of self-esteem as discussed in the section on the sample. The importance of these results must be tempered by the limitations imposed by differences in samples, cultural differences in interpretation of the questions and Western-oriented coverage of possible antecedents.

The three foci of adjustment could be distinguished, even though they shared considerable common variance, and there were substantial source effects; that is, correlations among measures from a common source (subject, teacher, or parent) tended to be higher than correlations among measures from different sources. The child's satisfaction with school correlated only marginally with teacher-judged academic performance, but at a similar level for both self-appraised academic performance and satisfaction with friends, so one might say that school adjustment had about equally strong academic and interpersonal aspects for the average student. Peer relations and academic performance bore not a negative relationship but rather a small positive relationship. Friendships and scholarship were not antagonistic concerns, neither were they particularly supportive of each other, overall. While it had been expected that attraction to family and school would be mutually supportive, and both antagonistic to peer attractions, this pattern did not emerge in the total sample to any substantial degree.

The role of the mediators

As we take a final look at the antecedents of adjustment and their mediators, the coping styles our respondents use in dealing with their adolescent world at home and at school, it is well to emphasize again that the variables we will discuss are those which remain a force when other significant correlates are also present. We will start our summary with the contribution of the coping style correlates to predicting academic adjustment. The most pervasive predictor of adjustment was self-esteem, with low hostility playing a significant role in adjustment to school and family, but not to friends, whereas low anxiety had a direct impact only on interpersonal adjustment. The students' academic value school means study maintained its significant contribution to satisfaction with school but to no other adjustment measure, even the academic performance scores.

Contributions from demographic information

The simplest bases for distinguishing among our adolescents are their and their parents' demographic characteristics, such as their sex, age and intellectual prowess. We also defined family composition as a demographic variable, as distinguished from our measures of the social characteristics of the family environment.

The sex of the respondent did not have a direct effect on any academic or family-adjustment measure. Though it proved to have a relationship with inter-personal adjustment, namely satisfaction with friends, the average relationship over the seven samples was not very high. The effect of gender was mediated by the personality variable of self-esteem, as reported by the child, but not the teacher, and by the teacher's ratings of hostility (males higher than females in both instances).

Older children tended to be less satisfied in general, but only dissatisfaction with school remains when considered with other social and demographic variables.

The marks the child received from the school, not surprisingly, had a direct effect on all measures of academic performance, regardless of source. In addition, marks had an indirect effect, through both self-reported and teacher-judged ratings of self-esteem (positive) on measures of academic performance and interpersonal competence.

Finally, parental and family characteristics showed no important universal relations with any kind of adjustment; hardly sustaining the belief held among some that single-parent families breed maladjustment in their children, or that only children tend to excel academically for there is no association between number of adults in the family and academic performance. There were cultural differences in parental education and minority-group status which did influence coping styles and adjustment, which we will come to soon.

Social antecedents

The family

One hypothesis about the effects of family on the child's ability to adapt is based on the notion that self-esteem reflects the influence of powerful others, in this case parents (Cheek and Hogan, 1983; Cooley, 1922; Mead, 1934). Of all the family characteristics, parental nurturance (as reported by the child) was most related to subjective satisfaction in all three domains of adjustment while the parent-judged punitiveness was a predictor of the parent's (low) evaluation of the child's academic performance, and parent-judged protectiveness was relevant only to the parent's satisfaction with the child's behaviour. In support of our hypothesis, the family's major effect on adjustment was indirect, with the most influential again being parental nurturance, which affected self-reported self-esteem and anxiety (negatively), and parental punitiveness (as reported by parents) which affected children's hostility.

A second framework in which family influence on children is placed proposes that children learn methods of coping by imitating parental role models (Miller and Dollard, 1946; Bandura, 1977). We examined the distribution of family roles as described by both our adolescents and their parents. There was remarkable consistency over samples, and between children and parents, in the factors which emerged. The two main factors were identified as status and maintenance roles. The status role cluster correlated with age, the maintenance role cluster with sex. When we looked at the relationship between family roles and adjustment or coping styles out of context (without the other variables present), we found children's participation in status roles was negatively correlated with parental protectiveness, both in the child's and the parent's eyes. Participation by the responding child in both status and maintenance roles was likely to be greatest in families with few adults. Maintenance roles were most likely to be performed by older females. However, when looking at the effects of family roles on adjustment in the context of other predictors, no direct or indirect effects were observed that were similar in all cultures. There were, however, the cultural norms on who performs status and maintenance roles in the family that did influence adjustment. We will come to those in the section on cultural effects.

When we look at the role allocation measures with significant correlates, age-role differentiation showed small negative relations with three measures of interpersonal adjustment (and three measures of family adjustment), suggesting that in families where parents and children performed different tasks, the children's adjustment, not only to the family but to peers as well, was likely to be impaired. With both school and interpersonal adjustment, sex-role differentiation was negatively related (at low levels) to all measures except the sociometric status score. However, as with the measures of types of roles filled by family members, when family role differentiation measures were entered into the regression equations along with other significant variables, no unique effect appeared. But, once again, the cultural norms on role diffusion did affect adjustment (see below).

The peers

Well-adjusted students are best able to select friends whose characteristics they share. These are likely to be demographic characteristics, such as sex and verbal ability; and academic performance as well as other levels of adjustment and personality characteristics displayed in the classroom such as self-confidence, hostility and anxiety. Though the degree of similarity in correlates varies over the several measures of adjustment, sociometric and other interpersonal measures are among the highest.

The influence of similarity to peers was primarily through the children selecting (or being selected by) classmates who resemble them on subjective satisfaction in all three measures of adjustment and/or coping measures themselves.

Note that this similarity is not only true for self-reported measures (child versus mean peer), but also for ratings of adjustment the child and his/her mean peer group received from the teacher on self-esteem and interpersonal competence and that the child and his/her mean peer group received from their parents on satisfaction with family. Though the fact that the same teacher rated all the classmates could result in similar ratings to those perceived as friends, having the same rater was not the cause of the similarity in parent's ratings of behaviour at home.

Attitudes

The importance our children placed on friends was mediated by hostility and school means study, and had a direct effect on the three interpersonal adjustment scores judged by the child, satisfaction with friends, interpersonal comfort and number of friends chosen to recreate with. Though both importance of friends and school affected all three adjustment areas when looked at alone, the only effect for importance of school common to all seven cultures was a negative one on school means study.

The culture

Cross-cultural correlations between predictors and dependent variables are often a mirror of within-cultural rs. In cultures where the average parental nurturance is high, children have higher self-esteem (both the child's and teacher's report). This was over and above the contribution made by the child being from a family with high nurturance. In addition, coming from cultures with low parental (over-) protectiveness (parental report) contributes to self-esteem. These findings seem to lend universal support to symbolic interactionism; high self-esteem grows in families with positive parental support reflected in high nurturance and low over-protectiveness and punitiveness, which go together. Cultures in which children regard their parents as generally nurturant tend to produce children with higher self-esteem, which, in turn, is associated with higher subjective and objective academic and interpersonal adjustment scores, than non-nurturant cultures.

However, there is another way to look at sample differences. Triandis (1997) notes that, with increased density, there is an increase in the influences of norms on behaviour. Our data, all collected at industrialized urban schools, show norms playing a significant role in predicting adjustment levels. Our samples differed on the level of parental education and the proportion of minority-group members. Cultures with a high level of parental education also had teachers who rated self-esteem high (and hostility low), and had parents who were more satisfied with the family according to both family adjustment measures. Though these variables did not make a significant contribution in the within-sample analyses, cultures who differ on these variables have different levels of adjustment associated with these characteristics of the sample.

Cultures who foster families *not* following traditional role assignments (by age and/or sex), also have cultures who report higher academic adjustment. Further, cultures where maintenance roles are not limited to only the mother also have both the child and the mother being happier with the child's behaviour. In cultures where mothers perform almost all maintenance functions, there may be a resentment of the child, as represented by lower parental satisfaction with the child's behaviour, and the child may not have enough interpersonal experience to make him/her feel comfortable when dealing with others outside the home (the interpersonal comfort measure of adjustment). Though the results are less dramatic for the role-modelling concept of family influence, there is some support for more successful adolescents coming from families where there is less rigid demographic restraint on role performers. In the future it will be important to determine the antecedents of these family characteristics in order to learn more about the family structure's effect on adjustment.

The cultural norm pertaining to the importance of friends not only had a direct effect on self-esteem and school means study (negative) it also contributed directly to all three areas of adjustment. Obviously, how much a culture values interpersonal relations has a bearing on adjustment. Now it is incumbent upon researchers to determine the antecedents of viewing friendships as important.

Implications for Future Research

Ideally differences in cultural means ought to lead to areas where refinement or development of new concepts will lead to further replication across cultures. This will then lead to an increase in the ability to predict adjustment levels, irrespective of the cultural context as the variables representing a culture's uniqueness are identified and included as a predictor of adjustment in all samples. Bronfenbrenner (1986) emphasizes the impact of the external characteristics of the environment on family practices. The implications of our cultural differences in parental practices and role diffusion variables, which lead to higher percentages of variance accounted for in measure of adjustment, again stresses the importance of learning more about the antecedents of these family measures.

At this stage in our field of cross-cultural social psychology, we obviously need to be thinking of other, important, variables to include in future studies to further interpret adjustment now represented by the unexplained variance, of which there is still a lot. There is variance associated with specific social environments, represented by the sample means. Already mentioned are the variables describing the effect of the social environment of the classroom itself on academic and interpersonal adjustment as highlighted by the high error terms for specific dependent variables which rely on peers' rating. In addition, there were unmeasured characteristics associated directly, and indirectly through mediators, with outcome measures. For instance, the unspecified variance attributed to Berlin represents unmeasured attributes directly affecting satisfaction with friends, whereas the mediator, self-reported anxiety, has significant predictors missing in the Canberra sample. These variables need to be identified and their effects replicated within other cultures. Refinement of the model to include these variables would not only increase our understanding of the factors contributing to satisfaction with friends, but would also aid in describing variables contributing to cultural differences in both the coping adaptation level and the adjustment to specific situations.

The fact that all our samples are from urbanized, industrialized areas limits the generality of the findings to similar samples; what predicts adolescent adjustment in more rural, third-world cultures remains to be seen. Rather than replicating Western industrial concepts, the next step should be to examine the possibility of identifying new variables in non-urban samples which could lead to increased accountability in predicting adjustment throughout the world, including adolescents in Occidental and Oriental cultures in urban and rural settings.

What does all this imply for future research? Primarily, the complexity of the results from our study obtained, from seven cultures, four sources of information and four domains of antecedents highlights the danger of generalizing from data which come from only one sample, only one data source and a narrow range of highly selected variables. Many assumptions of the universality of relationships between predictors and outcomes could not be substantiated when looked at in conjunction with other variables. For instance, in our study the roles family members take differed across samples, were reliably reported and were correlated with adjustment, but their significance was unimportant when other characteristics of the social environment were taken into account. However, they did suggest explanations for cultural differences as they provided an explanation for the samples' different levels of adjustment. Females' (but not males') self-esteem was negatively affected by parental (over-) protectiveness, however, when taken in context with the cultural norms, this becomes irrelevant. Though there certainly is a place for laboratory experiments in establishing measures and testing out hypothetical relationships, only by placing these variables in a field representing the spectrum of stimuli which play a part in a person's environment can we truly test out the effects of any one, or any one type, of variable on a nominated outcome.

Appendix: Scales

The exact wording of items assigned to each scale in all seven cultures are shown in this Appendix. The complete questionaires along with the culture specific descriptive statistics can be obtained by writing to the address given in the footnote to Chapter 2. Items without references are original to this study. Items preceded by an (R) were reverse scored.

Academic Performance

Child's report

1. (R) I am a rather poor student. (not true, true).
2. (R) How do you feel about your ability to do academic work? (very able, pretty able, somewhat able, not too able, not able at all) (Jessor and Jessor, 1984).

Parent's report

1. (R) How satisfied are you with this child's educational progress at the moment? (completely satisfied, very satisfied, fairly satisfied, a little dissatisfied, very dissatisfied) (Steinkalk, 1983).
2. (R) How do you feel about the quality of this child's school? (very good, fairly good, neither good nor bad, not very good, not good at all) (Campbell, Converse and Rodgers, 1976).
3. (R) How does this child feel about its studies? (loves them — looks forward to doing them, usually likes them, sometimes likes them and sometimes doesn't, usually doesn't like them).
4. How would you describe this child as a student? (hopeless, poor, indifferent, fair, good, outstanding).

Teacher's report

1. (R) How well does this student perform in classwork? (one of the best, definitely above average, about class average, definitely below average, one of the worst) (Taft and Cahill, 1981).
2. (R) Among all the students you have known, how would this student compare in academic performance? (outstanding — one of the best, well above

average, slightly above average, about average, slightly below average, well below average, very poor—one of the worst).

3.   Please describe this student by circling 1 (generally false) or 2 (generally true) for each statement: Alert in class.

Anxiety

Child's report (All items from Taylor, 1953)

1.   (R) I am happy most of the time. (not like me, like me).
2.   Life is a strain for me much of the time. (not like me, like me).
3.   At times I think I am no good at all. (not like me, like me).
4.   I tire quickly. (not like me, like me).
5.   I feel anxiety about someone or something almost all the time. (not like me, like me).
6.   I have periods of such great restlessness that I cannot sit long in a chair. (not like me, like me).
7.   I have sometimes felt that difficulties were piling up so high that I could not overcome them. (not like me, like me).
8.   I certainly am lacking in self-confidence. (not like me, like me).
9.   I certainly feel useless at times. (not like me, like me).
10.   I worry quite a bit over possible misfortunes (not like me, like me).
11.   I shrink from facing a crisis or difficulty. (not like me, like me).

Parent's report

1.   This child is upset (never, occasionally, sometimes, often, most of the time).
2.   Each person has a different way of showing tension. Which of the following describes this child? Put a tick if the child does this to some extent, two ticks if the child does it a lot. Leave a blank if doesn't apply.
       (a)   Worries about many things. (Rutter, 1967).
       (b)   Is afraid of new things. (Rutter, 1967).
       (c)   Cries easily. (Sines and Paulker, 1969).
       (d)   Often complains of aches and pains. (Rutter, 1967).

Teacher's report Please describe this student by circling 1 (generally false) or 2 (generally true) for each statement:

1.   Worries about many things. (Rutter, 1967).
2.   (R) Appears happy and carefree. (Rutter, 1967).

3. Becomes embarrassed easily. (Rutter, 1967).
4. Cries easily. (Sines and Paulker, 1969).
5. (R) Is rarely upset. (Sines and Paulker, 1969).

Hostility

Child's report

1. At times I feel like picking a fight with someone. (not like me, like me) (Caine, Foulds and Hope, 1967).
2. At times I feel like smashing things. (not like me, like me) (Caine, Foulds and Hope, 1967).

Parent's report

1. How would you describe this child's attitudes and behaviour at home? (circle all the words that apply).
   (a) Disobedient.
   (b) Hard to get along with.
   (c) Ill-tempered.
   (d) Bad manners.
2. This child talks back to its parents (never, seldom, sometimes, often, all the time).
3. This child is always getting into trouble. (generally false, generally true).
4. This child is often rebellious and disobedient. (generally false, generally true).
5. (R) This child behaves very well even without severe punishment. (generally false, generally true).
6. (R) This child never gets into trouble. (generally false, generally true).
7. Each person has a different way of showing tension. Which of the following describes this child? Put a tick beside the description if the child does this to some extent, and two ticks if the child does it a lot. Tick as many as applicable, but leave blank any description which does not apply to this child. Irritable — quick to 'fly off the handle' (generally false, generally true) (Rutter, 1967).
8. When you tell this child to do something, what is its usual response? (does it cheerfully, does it after some hesitation, argues back but usually does it, becomes sullen and hostile).
9. How often does this child act in ways you think aren't right? (never, rarely, sometimes, often, all the time).

Teacher's report

1. What is this student's general attitude toward authority? (always respectful, usually respectful, indifferent, often antagonistic, constantly combative).

2. When this student is told to do something by a teacher, what is the usual response? (does it cheerfully, does it after some hesitation, argues back but usually does it, becomes sullen and hostile).

3. (R) If there were no teacher around to watch this student, how would you expect him or her to behave? (irresponsible—untrustworthy, variable—can't tell—depends on what other children are doing, responsible—the same as if a teacher were there).

4. (R) Suppose adult authority and peer pressure were in conflict, how would you expect this student to respond? (follow peer pressure, be in conflict, follow adult authority).

5. Please describe this student by circling 1 (generally false) or 2 (generally true) for each statement: Is disruptive in class. (generally false, generally true) (McCabe, 1983).

6. Rubs people the wrong way. (generally false, generally true) (Wrigley et al., 1957).

7. Is irritable; quick to "fly off the handle." (generally false, generally true) (Rutter, 1967).

8. Talks back to the teacher. (generally false, generally true) (McCabe, 1983).

9. (R) Never gets into trouble. (generally false, generally true) (McCabe, 1983).

10. Provokes other students. (generally false, generally true) (McCabe, 1983).

Importance of Friends

Child's report

1. (R) Think of the relative importance of school, family, hobbies, *friends*, and so forth, in your life, write the number beside the most important and so on down to 8 beside the least important thing in your life: work, school, family, possessions and home, community, friends, leisure, the natural environment. Friends (Jessor and Jessor, 1984).

2. Would you say you spend quite a lot of time, a moderate amount of time, or relatively little time (none also provided):

   (a) (R) Talking with my friends.

   (b) (R) Entertaining my friends.

   (Scott and Scott, 1989)

3. When I want someone to talk to I go to a (circle as many as applicable.) . . . Friend (Scott and Scott, 1989).

Importance of School

Child's report

1. (R) Think of the relative importance of *school*, family, hobbies, friends, and

so forth, in your life, write the number beside the most important and so on down to 8 beside the least important thing in your life . . . School (Jessor and Jessor, 1984).

2. (R) Would you say you spend quite a lot of time, a moderate amount of time, or relatively little time (none also provided): Studying (Scott and Scott, 1989).

3. Which of the following statements come closest to how you feel about the need for education (doesn't matter, is alright, is pretty important, is one of the most important things in life for everyone).

4. How much education do you think people in this country should have as a minimum? (at least 6,9,12,15,18 years).

Interpersonal Comfort

Child's report

1. (R) How do you feel about the way you get on with other people? (delighted, pleased, mostly satisfied, neutral — neither satisfied nor dissatisfied, mixed — about equally satisfied and dissatisfied, mostly dissatisfied, unhappy, terrible) (Andrews and Withey, 1976).

2. (R) How interesting are you for other people? How interesting do they find you? They find me (very interesting, pretty interesting, somewhat interesting, not too interesting, not interesting at all) (Jessor and Jessor, 1984).

3. (R) How easy is it for you to make new friends? (very easy, easy, a little difficult, very difficult) (Jessor and Jessor, 1984).

4. (R) How easy is it for you to form meaningful relationships with members of your own sex? (very easy, fairly easy, not too easy, not easy at all) (Jessor and Jessor, 1977).

5. (R) How easy is it for you to form meaningful relationships with members of the opposite sex? (very easy, fairly easy, not too easy, not easy at all) (Jessor and Jessor, 1977).

6. (R) How easy is it to discuss things of a personal nature with your friends? (very easy, somewhat easy, somewhat difficult, very difficult) (Grichting, 1980).

Interpersonal Competence

Teacher's report

1. How does he or she fit into the class socially? (a loner, does not get on well with others, a good mixer, a leader) (Taft and Cahill, 1981).

2. How often has this student initiated a conversation with you? (never, occasionally, frequently, at every meeting).

3. How often have you seen this student in conversation with another student? (never, occasionally, frequently, all the time).

4.   (R) Do you get the impression that this student (feels quite at ease with others, feels at ease with most people, feels at ease with some but not with others, feels ill at ease but can carry on a conversation if necessary, is unable to relate to other people at all).

5.   Please describe this student by circling 1 (generally false) or 2 (generally true) for each statement:

   (a)   Gets along with everyone quite easily. (Scott and Scott, 1989).

   (b)   Is easy to talk to. (Wrigley et al., 1957).

   (c)   (R) Has few close friends. (Sines and Paulker, 1969).

Parental Nurturance

Child's report

1.   My father spoke to me with a warm and friendly voice. (completely false, somewhat false, somewhat true, completely true) (Parker et al., 1979).

2.   (R) My father did not help me as much as I needed. (completely false, somewhat false, somewhat true, completely true) (Parker et al., 1979).

3.   My father enjoyed talking things over with me. (completely false, somewhat false, somewhat true, completely true) (Parker et al., 1979).

4.   (R) My father made me feel I wasn't wanted. (completely false, somewhat false, somewhat true, completely true) (Parker et al., 1979).

5.   My father could make me feel better when I was upset. (completely false, somewhat false, somewhat true, completely true) (Parker et al., 1979).

6.   (R) My father did not praise me. (completely false, somewhat false, somewhat true, completely true) (Parker et al., 1979).

7.   (R) My father did not care what I did. (completely false, somewhat false, somewhat true, completely true).

8.   (R) My father was never around when I needed him. (completely false, somewhat false, somewhat true, completely true).

9.   My mother spoke to me with a warm and friendly voice. (completely false, somewhat false, somewhat true, completely true) (Parker et al., 1979).

10.   (R) My mother did not help me as much as I needed.(completely false, somewhat false, somewhat true, completely true) (Parker et al., 1979).

11.   My mother enjoyed talking things over with me. (completely false, somewhat false, somewhat true, completely true) (Parker et al., 1979).

12.   (R) My mother made me feel I wasn't wanted. (completely false, somewhat false, somewhat true, completely true) (Parker et al., 1979).

13. My mother could make me feel better when I was upset. (completely false, somewhat false, somewhat true, completely true) (Parker *et al.*, 1979).

14. (R) My mother did not praise me. (completely false, somewhat false, somewhat true, completely true) (Parker *et al.*, 1979).

15. (R) My mother did not care what I did. (completely false, somewhat false, somewhat true, completely true).

16. (R) My mother was never around when I needed her. (completely false, somewhat false, somewhat true, completely true).

Parent's report (Reluctance to punish — a priori scale)

1. I would never punish this child. (generally false, generally true).

2. What do you ordinarily do when this child misbehaves? (tick as many as applicable).

    (a) (R) Deprive the child of something it wants.

    (b) (R) Make the child do some extra work.

3. If you spank children, you do them more harm than good. (generally false, generally true).

Parental Protectiveness Control

Child's report

1. Difference score: "My father did not want me to grow up" *minus* "My father let me decide things for myself." (completely false, somewhat false, somewhat true, completely true) (items from Parker *et al.*, 1979).

2. Difference score: "My father felt I could not look after myself unless he was around" *minus* "My father gave me as much freedom as I wanted." (completely false, somewhat false, somewhat true, completely true) (items from Parker *et al.*, 1979).

3. Difference score: "My mother did not want me to grow up" *minus* "My mother let me decide things for myself." (completely false, somewhat false, somewhat true, completely true) (items from Parker *et al.*, 1979).

4. Difference score: "My mother felt I could not look after myself unless she was around" *minus* "My mother gave me as much freedom as I wanted." (completely false, somewhat false, somewhat true, completely true) (items from Parker *et al.*, 1979).

5. (R) My father let me do those things I like doing. (completely false, somewhat false, somewhat true, completely true) (Parker *et al.*, 1979).

6. (R) My mother let me do those things I like doing. (completely false, somewhat false, somewhat true, completely true) (Parker *et al.*, 1979).

7. If you wanted to go somewhere overnight with your friends, how would your parents feel about it? (they wouldn't care and I wouldn't bother to tell them, I would tell them but they would say it was alright, they would let me if they trusted the people I was going out with, they wouldn't let me go unless an adult they trusted were going along, they wouldn't let me go under any circumstances).

8. How do your parents feel about the clothes you wear? (they don't care and let me dress as I please, they want me to look nice but usually accept my taste, sometimes they approve and sometimes they disapprove of what I wear, they usually don't like my clothes and try to make me follow their tastes, they won't let me wear anything they don't like).

Parent's report – a priori scale

1. Difference score: "This child needs a good deal of supervision" *minus* "This child is given a great deal of freedom." (generally false, generally true).

2. Difference score: "This child has a hard time looking after itself" *minus* "This child is old enough to look after itself." (generally false, generally true).

3. At what age do you think children are old enough:
   (a)   to get a job for money outside the family?
   (b)   to decide what to wear and to buy their own clothing by themselves?
   (c)   to decide for themselves what sort of relationship to have with members of the opposite sex (including sexual relations).

Parental Punitiveness

Child's report

1. About how often do you get a thrashing? (never, once a year, once a month, once a week, almost every day).

2. My father often hit me. (completely false, somewhat false, somewhat true, completely true) (McCabe, 1983).

3. My mother often hit me. (completely false, somewhat false, somewhat true, completely true) (McCabe, 1983).

4. (R) My father wouldn't hurt me for anything. (completely false, somewhat false, somewhat true, completely true).

5. (R) My mother wouldn't hurt me for anything. (completely false, somewhat false, somewhat true, completely true).

Parent's report

1. What do you do when this child misbehaves? (tick as many as applicable).

(a)   Scold the child.

(b)   Spank the child.

2.   How often does this child get a good thrashing? (never, once a year, once a month, once a week, almost every day).

3.   I get angry with this child (never, rarely, sometimes, quite often, very often).

Satisfaction with Child's Behaviour

Parent's report

1.   How would you describe this child's attitudes and behaviour at home? (Circle all the words that apply).

(a)   Cooperative.

(b)   Mature.

(c)   Responsible.

Satisfaction with Family

Child's report

1.   (R) How do you feel about the things you and your family do together? (delighted, pleased, mostly satisfied, neutral—neither satisfied nor dissatisfied, mixed—about equally satisfied and dissatisfied, mostly dissatisfied, unhappy, terrible) (Andrews and Withey, 1976).

2.   (R) How do you feel about your family members' relations with each other? (delighted, pleased, mostly satisfied, neutral—neither satisfied nor dissatisfied, mixed—about equally satisfied and dissatisfied, mostly dissatisfied, unhappy, terrible) (Andrews and Withey, 1976).

3.   (R) Would you say that members of your family are (very close, pretty close, not too close, a little distant, pretty distant) (Jessor and Jessor, 1984).

4.   My home is a happy place to be. (generally false, generally true) (McCabe, 1983).

5.   My parents treat all children in the family fairly. (generally false, generally true) (McCabe, 1983).

Satisfaction with Family

Parent's report

1.   (R) All things considered, how satisfied are you with your family life? (delighted, pleased, mostly satisfied, neutral—neither satisfied nor dissatisfied, mixed—about equally satisfied and dissatisfied, mostly dissatisfied, unhappy, terrible) (Scott and Scott, 1989).

2.   (R) How do you feel about your children? (delighted, pleased, mostly

satisfied, neutral—neither satisfied nor dissatisfied, mixed—about equally satisfied and dissatisfied, mostly dissatisfied, unhappy, terrible) (Andrews and Withey, 1976).

3. (R) Are you happy with the sorts of friends your children have? (very happy, happy, not too happy, not happy at all) (Scott and Scott, 1989).

4. (R) How satisfied are you with the way you handle your role as parent? (very satisfied, satisfied, neither satisfied nor dissatisfied, dissatisfied, very dissatisfied) (Jessor and Jessor, 1984).

5. (R) How do you feel about the things you and your family do together? (delighted, pleased, mostly satisfied, neutral—neither satisfied nor dissatisfied, mixed—about equally satisfied and dissatisfied, mostly dissatisfied, unhappy, terrible) (Andrews and Withey, 1976).

6. (R) How do you feel about your family members' relations with each other? (delighted, pleased, mostly satisfied, neutral—neither satisfied nor dissatisfied, mixed—about equally satisfied and dissatisfied, mostly dissatisfied, unhappy, terrible) (Andrews and Withey, 1976).

7. (R) Would you say that members of your family are: (very close, fairly close, not too close, a little distant, quite distant) (Jessor and Jessor, 1977).

8. Our home is a happy place to be (generally false, generally true) (McCabe, 1983).

Satisfaction with Friends
Child's report

1. (R) Are you happy with the sorts of friends you have here? (very happy, happy, not too happy, not happy at all) (Scott and Scott, 1989).

2. (R) How do you feel about the way other people treat you? (delighted, pleased, mostly satisfied, neutral—neither satisfied nor dissatisfied, mixed—about equally satisfied and dissatisfied, mostly dissatisfied, unhappy, terrible) (Andrews and Withey, 1976).

3. (R) Many of the students here are selfish and inconsiderate. (not true, true) (Bradburn, 1969).

Satisfaction with School
Child's report

1. (R) How satisfied are you with your school here? (completely satisfied, very satisfied, fairly satisfied, a little dissatisfied, very dissatisfied).

2. (R) If you had a choice, would you prefer to go to this school or some other school?

3. Which of the following statements comes closest to the way you feel about

this school? (I hate this school, I don't like this school very much and would rather not be here, this school is OK but I'd rather be somewhere else, this school is pretty good, this school is great—I would rather be here than anywhere else).

4. (R) How do you feel about your studies? (I enjoy them, they are OK, mostly boring, I hate them).

5. (R) How important for your future are the things your teachers are trying to teach you? (very important, quite important, not very important, not important at all).

6. (R) How interesting do the teachers make the classwork? (very interesting, fairly interesting, not very interesting, very boring).

School Means Study

Child's report—not interpersonal

1. Which of the following things are most important to you in school? Write a number 1 beside the most important thing, the number 2 beside the next most important thing, and so on down to 9 for the least important thing in school.

    (a) (R) Studying.

    (b) (R) Doing what the teachers want me to do.

    (c) The friends I have here.

    (d) The fun I have playing.

School Means Study

Parent's report—not interpersonal

1. From your point of view, which of the following things should be most important to your child at school? Write a number 1 beside the most important thing, the number 2 beside the next most important thing, and so on down to 9 for the least important thing in this child's school.

    (a) (R) Doing what the teachers want.

    (b) (R) Trying to get good marks.

    (c) Learning to play sports.

    (d) Getting along with other children.

Self-esteem

Child's report

1. (R) How do you feel about the way you handle the problems that come up in your life? (delighted, pleased, mostly satisfied, neutral—neither satisfied nor

dissatisfied, mixed—about equally satisfied and dissatisfied, mostly dissatisfied, unhappy, terrible) (Andrews and Withey, 1976).

2. (R) How do you feel about yourself? (delighted, pleased, mostly satisfied, neutral—neither satisfied nor dissatisfied, mixed—about equally satisfied and dissatisfied, mostly dissatisfied, unhappy, terrible) (Andrews and Withey, 1976).

3. (R) How do you feel about what you are accomplishing in life? (delighted, pleased, mostly satisfied, neutral—neither satisfied nor dissatisfied, mixed—about equally satisfied and dissatisfied, mostly dissatisfied, unhappy, terrible) (Andrews and Withey, 1976).

4. (R) How competent do you feel you are to do the things you are really interested in? (very competent, fairly competent, not too competent, not competent at all) (Jessor and Jessor, 1977).

Teacher's report

1. Is well adjusted. (generally false, generally true) (Crabbe and Scott, 1972).

2. (R) Lacks confidence in own opinions. (generally false, generally true) (Wrigley *et al.*, 1957).

3. Is not afraid of making mistakes. (generally false, generally true) (Ross, Lacey and Parton, 1965).

4. Is self-confident. (generally false, generally true) (Ross, Lacey and Parton, 1965).

5. Is sure of himself or herself. (generally false, generally true).

6. Is reluctant to perform in front of others. (generally false, generally true).

References

Abadzi, H. (1984). Ability grouping effects on academic achievement and self-esteem in a southwestern school district. *Journal of Educational Research*, **77**, 287–292.

Achenbach, T. M., McConaughy, S. H. and Howell, C. T. (1987). Child/adolescent behavioral and emotional problems: implications of cross-informant correlations for situational specificity. *Psychological Bulletin*, **101**, 213–232.

Allan, G. (1985). *Family Life: Domestic Roles and Social Organisation*, Oxford: Basil Blackwell.

Allen, W. R. (1988). Black students in U.S. higher education: toward improved access, adjustment, and achievement. *Urban Review*, **20**, 165–188.

Amato, P. (1990). Dimensions of the family environment as perceived by children: a multidimensional scaling analysis. *Journal of Marriage and the Family*, **52**, 613–620.

Andrews, F. M. and Withey, S. B. (1976). *Social Indicators of Well-Being: Americans' Perceptions of Life Quality*, NY: Plenum.

Back, K. W. (1951). The exertion of influence through social communication. *Journal of Abnormal and Social Psychology*, **46**, 9–23.

Bahr, H. M. and Martin, T. K. (1983). "And thy neighbor as thy self": self-esteem and faith in people as correlates of religiosity and family solidarity among Middletown high school students. *Journal for the Scientific Study of Religion*, **22**, 132–144.

Bandura, A. (1977). *Social Learning Theory*, Englewood Cliffs, NJ: Prentice-Hall.

Baron, R. M. and Kenny, D. A. (1986). The moderator—mediator variable distinction in social psychological research: conceptual, strategic and statistical considerations. *Journal of Personality and Social Psychology*, **51**, 1173–1182.

Benedict, R. (1946). *The Chrysanthemum and the Sword: Patterns of Japanese Culture*, Boston: Houghton-Mifflin.

Berndt, T. J. (1989). Influences of friendship on changes in students' adjustment during a school year. *Biennial Meeting of the Society for Research in Child Development*, Kansas City.

Berry, J. W. (1980). Acculturation as varieties of adaptation. In Padilla, A. M. (ed.), *Acculturation: Theory, Models and Some New Findings*, Boulder, CO: Westview Press, 9–23.

Berry, J. W. and Kim, U. (1988). Acculturation and mental health. In Dasen, P., Berry, J. W. and Sartorius, N. (eds), *Cross-Cultural Psychology and Health: Towards Applications*, London: Sage.

Bharadwaj, R. (1985). Scientific achievement as determined by adjustment, social interest and sex. *Indian Journal of Psychometry and Education*, **16**, 25—30.

Boehnke, K. (1996). *Is Intelligence Negligible?: The Relationship of Family Climate and School Behavior in a Cross-Cultural Perspective*, Munster/NY: Waxmann.

Boucher, J. and Osgood, C. E. (1969). The Pollyanna hypothesis. *Journal of Verbal Learning and Verbal Behaviour*, **8**, 1—8.

Bradburn, N. M. (1969). *The Structure of Psychological Well-Being*, Chicago: Aldine.

Broman, C. L. (1988). Household work and family life satisfaction of Blacks. *Journal of Marriage and the Family*, **50**, 743—748.

Bronfenbrenner, U. (1970). Reaction to social pressure from adults versus peers among Soviet day school and boarding school pupils in the perspective of an American sample. *Journal of Personality and Social Psychology*, **15**, 179—189.

—————— (1986). Ecology of the family as a context for human development. *Developmental Psychology*, **22**, 723—742.

Caine, T. M., Foulds, G. A. and Hope, K. (1967). *Manual of the Hostility and Direction of Hostility Questionnaire*, London: University of London Press.

Campbell, A., Converse, P. E. and Rodgers, W. L. (1976). *The Quality of American Life*, NY: Russell Sage.

Campbell, D. T. and Fiske, D. A. (1959). Convergent and discriminant validity by the multitrait-multimethod matrix. *Psychological Bulletin*, **56**, 81—105.

Cattell, R. B. (1993). What's wrong with psychology? *The Psychologist*, January, 22—23.

Cheek, J. M. and Hogan, R. (1983). Self-concepts, self-preservations, and moral judgments. In Suls, J. and Greenwald, A. G. (eds), *Perspectives on the Self* (Vol. 2), Hillsdale, NJ: Lawrence Erlbaum, 249—273.

Chen, C., Lee, S. and Stevenson, H. W. (1995). Response style and cross-cultural comparisons of rating scales among East Asian and North American students. *Psychological Science*, **6**, 170—175.

Cierkonski, Z. (1975). Studies of learning difficulties in nervous adolescents in secondary school. *Psychologia Wychowawczai*, **18**, 703—713.

Clark, L., Gresham, F. M. and Elliott, S. N. (1985). Development and validation of a social skills assessment measure: the TROSS—C. *Journal of Psychoeducational Assessment*, **3**, 347—356.

Coleman, J. S. (1961). *The Adolescent Society: The Social Life of the Teenager and its Impact on Education*, NY: Free Press.

Compas, B. E., Howell, D. C., Phares, V., Williams, R. A. and Ledoux, N. (1989).

Parent and child stress and symptoms: an integrative analysis. *Developmental Psychology*, **25**, 550–559.

Cooley, C. H. (1922). *Human Nature and the Social Order*, NY: Scribner.

Coopersmith, S. (1967). *Antecedents of Self-Esteem*, San Francisco: Freeman.

Crabbe, J. and Scott, W. A. (1972). Academic and personal adjustment. *Journal of Counselling Psychology*, **19**, 58–64.

Cronbach, L. J. (1951). Coefficient alpha and the internal structure of tests. *Psychometrika*, **16**, 297–334.

Crosby, F. J. (ed.) (1987). *Spouse, Parent, Worker: On Gender and Multiple Roles*, New Haven: Yale University Press.

Damon, W. and Hart, D. (1982). The development of self-understanding from infancy through adolescence. *Child Development*, **53**, 841–864.

Darom, E. and Rich, Y. (1988). Sex differences in attitudes toward school: student self-reports and teacher perceptions. *British Journal of Educational Psychology*, **58**, 350–355.

Dunnigan, T., McNall, M. and Mortimer, J. T. (1993). The problem of metaphorical nonequivalence in cross-cultural survey research. *Journal of Cross-Cultural Psychology*, **24**(3), 344–365.

Emery, R. E. (1982). Interparental conflict and the children of discord and divorce. *Psychological Bulletin*, **92**, 310–330.

Epstein, J. L. (1989). The selection of friends. In Berndt, T. J. and Ladd, G. W. (eds), *Peer Relationships in Child Development*, NY: Wiley, 158–187.

———— and McPartland, J. M. (1977a). *Family and School Interactions and Main Effects on Affective Outcomes* (Report No. 235), Baltimore: John Hopkins U., Center for Social Organization of Schools.

———— and———— (1977b). *Sex Differences in Family and School Influence on Student Outcomes* (Report No. 236), Baltimore: John Hopkins U., Center for Social Organization of Schools.

Estes, R. (1973). Determinants of differential stress levels among university students. *Journal of the American College Health Association*, **21**, 470–476.

Feldman, S. S. and Elliott, G. R. (eds) (1990). *At the Threshold: The Developing Adolescent*, Cambridge, MA: Harvard University Press.

Festinger, L., Schachter, S. and Back, K. W. (1963). *Social Pressures in Informal Groups: A Study of Human Factors in Housing*, London: Tavistock. (original work published 1950)

Fisher, R. A. (1941). *Statistical Methods for Research Workers* (8th rev. edn), Edinburgh: Oliver & Boyd.

Frankenhauser, M. (1983). The sympathetico-adrenal and pituitary-adrenal response to challenge: comparison between the sexes. In Dembrowski, T. M., Schmidt T. H. and Blumchen, G. M. (eds), *Behavioural Bases of Coronary Heart Disease*, Basel: S. Karger, 91–105.

Furnham, A. and Gunter, B. (1989). *The Anatomy of Adolescence: Young People's Social Attitudes in Britain*, London: Routledge.

Gavin, L. and Furman, W. (1989). Age differences in adolescents' perceptions and their peer groups. *Developmental Psychology*, **25**, 827–834.

Goodman, S. H. and Brumley, H. E. (1990). Schizophrenic and depressed mothers: relational deficits in parenting. *Developmental Psychology*, **26**, 31–39.

Grichting, W. (1980). *Questionnaire: Alcoholism and Its Prevention in Townsville*, Townsville, Australia: James Cook University, Behavioural Sciences Department.

Griswold, P. A. (1980). Family outing activities and achievement among fourth graders in compensatory education funded schools. *Journal of Educational Research*, **79**, 261–266.

Haas, L. (1981). Domestic role sharing in Sweden. *Journal of Marriage and the Family*, **43**, 957–967.

Hammen, C., Burge, D. and Stansbury, K. (1990). Relationship of mother and child variables for child outcomes in a high-risk sample: a causal modeling analysis. *Developmental Psychology*, **26**, 24–30.

Hardesty, C. and Bokemeier, J. (1989). Finding time and making do: distribution of household labor in non-metropolitan marriages. *Journal of Marriage and the Family*, **51**, 253–267.

Heider, F. (1958). *The psychology of interpersonal relations*, NY: John Wiley & Sons.

Henderson, A. S., Byrne, D. G. and Duncan-Jones, P. (1981). *Neurosis and the Social Environment*, Sydney: Academic Press.

Hofstede, G. (1980). *Culture's Consequences: International Differences in Work Related Values*, Beverly Hills, CA: Sage Publications.

Hunt, D. E., Butler, L. F., Noy, J. E. and Rosser, M. (1977). *Assessment of Conceptual Level by the Paragraph Completion Method*, Toronto: Ontario Institute for Studies in Education.

Ide, J. K., Parkerson, J., Haertel, G. D. and Walberg, H. J. (1981). Peer group influence on educational outcomes: a qualitative synthesis. *Journal of Educational Psychology*, **73**, 472–484.

Jessor, R. (1993). Successful adolescent development among youth in high risk settings. *American Psychologist*, **48**, 117–126.

—— and Jessor, S. L. (1977). *Problem Behavior and Psycho-Social Development: A Longitudinal Study of Youth*, New York: Academic Press.

—— and—— (1984). Adolescence to young adulthood: a twelve-year prospective study of problem behavior and psycho-social development. In Mednick, S. A., Harway, M. and Finello, K. M. (eds), *Handbook of Longitudinal Research, Vol. 2: Teenage and Adult Cohorts*, NY: Praeger.

Kandel, D. B., Davies, M. and Baydar, N. (1990). The creation of interpersonal contexts: homophily in dyadic relationships in adolescence and young adulthood. In Robins, L. N. and Rutter, M. (eds), *Straight and Devious Pathways from Childhood to Adulthood*, Cambridge: Cambridge University Press, 221—241.

—— and Lesser, G. S. (1972). *Youth in Two Worlds*, San Francisco: Jossey-Bass.

Kardiner, A. (1945). *The Psychological Frontiers of Society*, NY: Columbia University Press.

Kumawat, U. (1985). A study of certain factors related with high and low achievement in college students. *Asian Journal of Psychology and Education*, **15**, 1—7.

Lackovic-Grgin, K. and Dekovic, M. (1990). The contribution of significant others to adolescents' self-esteem. *Adolescence*, **25**, 839—846.

Lamborn, S. D., Dornbusch, S. M. and Steinberg, L. (1996). Ethnicity and community context as moderators of the relations between family decision making and adolescent adjustment. *Child Development*, **67**, 283—301.

Leung, K. and Bond, M. H. (1989). On the empirical identification of dimensions for cross-cultural comparisons. *Journal of Cross-Cultural Psychology*, **20**, 133—151.

Levine, M. (1977). Sex differences in behavior ratings: male and female teachers rate male and female pupils. *American Journal of Community Psychology*, **5**, 347—353.

Lewin, K. (1936). *Principles of Topological Psychology*, NY and London: McGraw-Hill.

Lopez, F. G. (1987). The impact of parental divorce on college student development. *Journal of Counselling and Development*, **65**, 484—486.

Loranger, M., Verret, C. and Arsenault, R. (1986). Les enseignants et les conduites sociales de leurs eleves. *Canadian Journal of Behavioural Science*, **18**, 257—269.

Maccoby, E. E. and Martin, J. A. (1983). Socialization in the context of the family parent—child interactions. In Mussen, P. H. (ed.), *Handbook of Child Psychology* (4th edn.), Vol. 4, NY: Wiley.

Mackinnon, A. J., Henderson, A. S. and Andrews, G. (1991). The parental bonding instrument: a measure of perceived or actual behavior? *Acta Psychiatrica Scandinavia*, **83**, 153—159.

Markus, H. R. and Kitayama, S. (1991). Culture and the self: implications for cognition, emotion, and motivation. *Psychological Review*, **98**, 224—253.

McCabe, M. (1983). Personality and family background of high-school counselees. Unpublished honours thesis, The Australian National University, Canberra, Australia.

McClure, R. F. (1974). Multivariate identification and prediction of university student problems. *The Journal of Experimental Education*, **42**, 44—49.

McCord, W. J., McCord, J. and Howard, A. (1961). Familial correlates of aggression in nondelinquent male children. *Journal of Abnormal and Social Psychology*, **62**, 79—93.

McCrae, R. R. and Costa, P. T., Jr. (1988a). Recalled parent—child relations and adult personality. *Journal of Personality*, **56**, 417—434.

—— and—— (1988b). Do parental influences matter? *Journal of Personality*, **56**, 445—449.

McPartland, J. M. and Epstein, J. L. (1975). *An Investigation of the Interaction of Family and School Factors in Open-School Effects on Students* (Report No. 192), Baltimore: John Hopkins U., Center for Social Organization of Schools.

Mead, G. H. (1934). *Mind, Self, and Society*, Chicago: University of Chicago Press.

Mead, M. (1943). *Coming of Age in Somoa: A Study of Adolescence and Sex in Primitive Societies*, NY: Morrow. Harmondsworth Middlesex: Penguin Books. (original work published 1928).

Mechanic, D. and Hansell, S. (1989). Divorce, family conflict, and adolescents' well-being. *Journal of Health and Social Behavior*, **30**, 105—116.

Mehta, G. S. (1983). Adjustment and personality types among obedient, disobedient students. *Indian Psychological Review*, **24**, 38—41.

Midgley, C. and Feldlaufer, H. (1987). Students' and teachers' decision-making fit before and after the transition to junior high school. *Journal of Early Adolescence*, **7**, 225—241.

Miller, N. E. and Dollard, J. W. (1941). *Social Learning and Imitation*, New Haven: Yale University Press.

Miller, K. E. and Park, K. (1989). Adolescents' perceptions of friends' and parents' influence on aspects of their school adjustment. *Journal of Early Adolescence*, **9**, 419—435.

Mitchell, C. and Greschuck, D. (1982). Self-concept and identification of students needing a counselling center. *Psychological Reports*, **50**, 487—490.

Murdock, G. P. *et al.* (1938, 1st edn.) Outline of Cultural Materials. In *Behavior Science Outlines*, Vol. 1, New Haven: Institute of Human Relations, Yale University.

Newcomb, T. M. (1961). *The Acquaintance Process*. NY: Holt, Rinehart and Winston.

Ohannessian, C. M., Lerner, R. M., Lerner, J. V. and von Eye, A. (1994). A longitudinal study of perceived family adjustment and emotional adjustment in early adolescence. *Journal of Early Adolescence*, **3**, 371—390.

Oliver, M. L., Rodriguez, C. J. and Mickelson, R. A. (1985). Brown and Black in White: the social adjustment and academic performance of Chicano and Black students in a predominantly White university. *Urban Review*, **17**, 3—24.

Olson, D. H., McCubbin, H. I., Barnes, H., Larson, A., Muxen, M. and Wilson, M. (1983). *Families: What Makes Them Work*, Beverly Hills, CA: Sage Publications.

Pandey, H. (1977). Adjustment between bright and average intermediate adolescents: a comparative study. *Indian Educational Review*, **12**, 86—90.

Parker, G. (1983). *Parental Overprotection: A Risk Factor in Psychosocial Development*, NY: Grune & Stratton.

——— (1989). The Parental Bonding Instrument: psychometric properties reviewed. *Psychiatric Developments*, **4**, 317—335.

——— and Barnett, B. (1988). Perceptions of parenting in childhood and social support in adulthood. *American Journal of Psychiatry*, **145**, 479—482.

——— Tupling, H. and Brown, L. B. (1979). A parental bonding instrument. *British Journal of Medical Psychology*, **52**, 1—10.

Parsons, T. and Bales, R. F. (1955). *Family: Socialization and Interaction Process*. Glencoe, Illinois: Free Press.

Petersen, A. C. (1988). Adolescent development. *Annual Review of Psychology*, **39**, 583—607.

——— and Hamburg, B. A. (1986). Adolescence: a developmental approach to problems and psychotherapy. *Behavioral Therapy*, **17**, 480—499.

Poirier, P. P., Tetreau, B. and Strobel, M. (1979). Adjustment and self-esteem of users and nonusers of a university counselling service. *Canadian Counsellor*, **13**, 140—146.

Poortinga, Y. H. and Malpass, R. S. (1986). Making inferences from cross-cultural data. In Lonner, W. J. and Berry, J. W. (eds), *Field Methods in Cross-Cultural Research*, Beverly Hills, California: Sage Publications.

Raphael, D. (1988). High school conceptual level as an indicator of young adult adjustment. *Journal of Personality Assessment*, **52**, 679—690.

Rexroat, C. and Shehan, C. (1987). The family life cycle and spouses' time in housework. *Journal of Marriage and the Family*, **49**, 737—750.

Ross, A. O., Lacey, H. M. and Parton, D. A. (1965). The development of a behavior checklist for boys. *Child Development*, **36**, 1013—1027.

Rutter, M. (1967). A children's behaviour questionnaire for completion by teachers: preliminary findings. *Journal of Child Psychology and Psychiatry and Allied Disciplines*, **8**, 1—11.

——— (1985). Family and school influences on behavioural development. *Journal of Child Psychology and Psychiatry*, **26**, 349—368.

——— (1990). Commentary: some focus and process considerations regarding effects of parental depression on children. *Developmental Psychology*, **26**, 60—67.

——— Yule, B., Quinton, D., Rowlands, O., Yule, W. and Berger, M. (1975). Attainment and adjustment in two geographical areas: III—some factors accounting for area differences. *British Journal of Psychiatry*, **125**, 520—533.

Ryba, K. A., Edelman, L. and Chapman, J. W. (1984). Academic self concept and personal adjustment of work-experience class students. *Australia and New Zealand Journal of Developmental Disabilities*, **10**, 197—202.

Santrock, J. W. and Tracy, R. L. (1978). Effects of children's family structure status on the development of stereotypes by teachers. *Journal of Educational Psychology*, **70**, 754—757.

Sarason, I. G., Sarason, B. R. and Shearin, E. N. (1986). Social support as an individual difference variable: its stability, origins, and relational aspects. *Journal of Personality and Social Psychology*, **50**, 845—855.

Scherer, K. R. (ed.) (1988). *Facets of Emotion: Recent Research*, Hillsdale, NJ: Erlbaum.

—— Wallbott, H. G. and Summerfield, A. B. (eds) (1986). *Experiencing Emotion: A Cross-Cultural Study*, Cambridge: Cambridge University Press.

Scott, W. A. (1960). Measures of test homogeneity. *Educational and Psychological Measurement*, **20**, 751—758.

—— (1965). *Values and Organizations: A Study of Fraternities and Sororities*, Chicago: Rand McNally.

—— and Cohen, R. D. (1978a). Assessing norms and practices of families, schools, and peer groups. *Australian and New Zealand Journal of Sociology*, **14**, 173—180.

—— and—— (1978b). Sociometric indices of group structure. *Australian Journal of Psychology*, **30**, 41—57.

—— and Peterson, C. (1975). Adjustment, pollyannaism, and attraction to close relationships. *Journal of Consulting and Clinical Psychology*, **43**, 872—880.

—— and Scott, R. (1979). Structural properties of groups. *Australian Journal of Psychology*, **31**, 89—100.

—— and—— (1989). *Adaptation of Immigrants: Individual Differences and Determinants*, Oxford: Pergamon Press.

—— and—— (1991). Adaptation of immigrant and native-born Australians. *Australian Psychologist*, **26**, 43—48.

——, ——, and McCabe, M. (1991). Family relationships and children's personality: a cross-cultural, cross-source comparison. *British Journal of Social Psychology*, **30**, 1—20.

——, ——, Boehnke, K., Cheng, S., Leung, K. and Sasaki, M. (1991). Children's personality as a function of family relations within and between cultures. *Journal of Cross-Cultural Psychology*, **22**, 182—208.

Sears, R. R., Maccoby, E. E. and Levin, H. (1957). *Patterns of Child Rearing*, Evanston: Row, Peterson.

Segall, M. H. (1979). *Cross-Cultural Psychology: Human Behavior in Global Perspective*, Monterey, CA: Brooks/Cole.

Shweder, R. A. (1973). Cross-cultural research. *Ethos*, **1**, 531—545.

Silverberg, S. B. and Steinberg, L. (1990). Psychological well-being of parents with early adolescent children. *Developmental Psychology*, **26**, 658—666.

Sines, J. O. and Paulker, J. D. (1969). Identification of clinically relevant dimensions of children's behavior. *Journal of Consulting and Clinical Psychology*, **33**, 728—734.

Skaalvik, E. M. and Hagtvet, K. A. (1990). Academic achievement and self-concept: an analysis of causal predominance in a developmental perspective. *Journal of Personality and Social Psychology*, **58**, 292—307.

Slater, E. J. and Haber, J. D. (1984). Adolescent adjustment following divorce as a function of familial conflict. *Journal of Consulting and Clinical Psychology*, **52**, 920—921.

————, Stewart, K. J. and Linn, M. W. (1983). The effect of family disruption on adolescent males and females. *Adolescence*, **18**, 931—942.

Smith, P.B. and Bond, M. H. (1993). *Social Psychology Across Cultures: Analysis and Perspectives*, NY: Harvester Wheatsheaf.

Steinberg, L., Elmen, J. and Mounts, N. (1989). Authoritative parenting, psychosocial maturity, and academic success among adolescents. *Child Development*, **60**, 1424—1436.

Steinkalk, E. (1983). The Adaptation of Soviet Jews in Victoria: A Study of Adolescent Immigrants and Their Parents. Unpublished doctoral dissertation, Monash University, Melbourne, Australia.

Strodtbeck, F. L. (1964). Considerations of meta-method in cross-cultural studies. *American Anthropologist*, **66**, 223—229.

Taft, R. and Bodi, M. (1980). A study of language competence and first language maintenance in bilingual children. *International Review of Applied Psychology*, **29**, 173—182.

———— and Cahill, D. (1981). Education of immigrants in Australia. In Bhatnager, J. (ed.), *Educating Immigrants*, NY: St Martin's Press, 16—46.

Takac, R. and Benyamini, K. (1989). Criteria for children's adjustment in school, peer group and youth movement. *School Psychology International*, **10**, 257—263.

Taylor, J. A. (1953). A personality scale of manifest anxiety. *Journal of Abnormal and Social Psychology*, **48**, 285—290.

Thomas, W. I. and Znaniecki, F. (1958). *The Polish Peasant in Europe and America* (5 vols.). Boston: Badger; NY: Dover. (original work published 1919)

Triandis, H. C. (1997). A cross-cultural perspective on social psychology. In McGarty, C. and Haslam, S. A. (Eds) *The Message of Social Psychology: Perspectives on Mind in Society*, Oxford: Blackwell.

————*et al.* (eds) (1980). *Handbook of Cross-Cultural Psychology* (6 vols.), Boston: Allyn and Bacon.

Wagner, B. M. and Compas, B. E. (1990). Gender, instrumentality, and expressivity: moderators of the relation between stress and psychological symptoms during adolescence. *American Journal of Community Psychology*, **18**, 383—406.

Waldo, M. (1984). Roommate communication as related to students' personal and social adjustment. *Journal of College Student Personnel*, **25**, 39—44.

Wall, R. C. and Pryzwansky, W.B. (1985). Secondary teacher and mental health professional views of students with school adjustment problems. *Professional Psychology Research and Practice*, **16**, 881—888.

Whiting, J. W. M. and Child, I. L. (1953). *Child Training and Personality*, New Haven: Yale University Press.

Williamson, R. C. (1977). Variables in adjustment and life goals among high school students. *Adolescence*, **12**, 213—225.

Wrigley, C., Cherry, C. N., Lee, M. C. and McQuitty, L. L. (1957). Use of the square-root method to identify factors in the job performance of aircraft mechanics. *Psychological Monographs: General and Applied*, **71**, 1—28.

Youngblood, R. L. (1976). Self-esteem and academic achievement of Filipino high school students. *Educational Research Quarterly*, **1**, 27—36.

Index